World Building For Writers: Create Unique Settings with Consistent Rules and Rich Details

PUBLISHED BY Maya Linden

Table of contents

Introduction — Designing Worlds That Generate Story

World-building is often misunderstood. Many writers approach it as a decorative exercise—sketching maps, listing noble houses, inventing currencies or magical plants, and then hoping these fragments will somehow cohere into a believable setting. But good world-building doesn't emerge from accumulation. It comes from design—deliberate, constrained, and purposeful design. A world is not a scrapbook of clever ideas; it is a system, and that system's rules should yield friction, possibility, and story. This book is not about making worlds *look* real—it's about making them *behave* real. When a setting is constructed correctly, it becomes a pressure chamber that shapes characters, defines their dilemmas, and generates storylines that could only happen *there*.

Imagine your fictional world as a machine that runs on tension. The geography, politics, climate, economy, and metaphysics are not decorations—they are the gears and levers that determine what your characters can and cannot do, what they must sacrifice, and how they rationalize their place in the larger system. If you think like an engineer rather than a tourist, your settings will gain gravity. Instead of being a backdrop for events, they will *cause* them. A reader may not consciously analyze your trade routes or religious taboos, but they will feel when every part of the world pushes logically against the others. That internal consistency creates trust. It tells the reader: "This place is real enough to matter."

What This Book Isn't

This isn't a rehash of world-building's usual trinity—culture, map, and magic. It isn't another invitation to spend weeks naming mountain ranges or inventing your own calendar before you've written a single scene. Those things can be valuable, but only after the deeper structure is in place. Instead, this book treats world-building as a dynamic system—an engine that must continue functioning even when characters stress it to its limits.

Every method you'll encounter here aims at one thing: *consequence*. If a rule exists in your world, it must ripple through behavior, institutions, and individual choice. A climate of perpetual dusk doesn't just color the sky; it alters agriculture, circadian rhythms, and the psychology of faith. A resource that extends life changes inheritance law, religion, and warfare. A teleportation spell rewrites the economics of distance and trust. You can trace every memorable story down to such interactions between a rule and its inevitable fallout.

That's why this book avoids encyclopedic filler. You won't find massive lists of invented species or sample pantheons here. Instead, you'll learn frameworks—repeatable processes that let you generate new worlds with coherence and personality each time. These frameworks are not for show; they're for storytelling. The goal is not to build one perfect world, but to develop a toolkit that can support *many*. Whether you're writing epic fantasy, near-future sci-fi, literary magical realism, or alt-history noir, the same design logic applies. Systems are portable; lore is not. Once you master the logic of systems, you'll never again be trapped by your own lore.

The difference between a forgettable fantasy and a gripping one often comes down to this: does the world merely *exist*, or does it *respond*? Passive worlds are wallpaper. Active worlds—those with built-in constraints and consequences—generate drama without you having to force it. They provide natural resistance, the same way gravity gives shape to flight. That's what this book helps you engineer.

The Constraints-First Mindset

The most powerful worlds begin not with abundance but with constraint. A blank page feels like freedom, but in practice, it's paralysis. The moment you start to impose limits, creative pressure builds. A setting designed around scarcity—of water, time, energy, information, or legitimacy—immediately develops texture. The human condition emerges when people are forced to trade one necessity for another.

Think of your world's rules as falling into three categories: invariants, dials, and experiments. **Invariants** are the non-negotiables—the physical or metaphysical laws that can't be broken without rewriting the entire world. They're the foundation stones. **Dials** are the variables that can shift within a range, such as social tolerance, political stability, or resource distribution. Turning these dials alters tone and tension. **Experiments** are the speculative elements—the new technologies, ideologies, or species that test the boundaries of the existing system. By classifying your ideas this way, you prevent the mushy, hand-wavy logic that plagues many ambitious settings.

A world that feels "real" isn't one that explains everything; it's one that behaves predictably under pressure. When you introduce a rule, immediately test its edge cases. What breaks? Who exploits the loopholes? What does this rule make impossible that would otherwise seem obvious? The way your inhabitants respond to those limits is what gives your setting its moral and emotional reality. The medieval peasant who can't legally hunt because forests belong to nobles, the astronaut who knows faster-than-light travel causes temporal dislocation, the priest whose god answers only once in a lifetime—these people live inside systems that constrain and define them. And those constraints, properly designed, become narrative fuel.

Start from tension, not trivia. Instead of inventing endless detail, ask what your world's inhabitants *can't* do—and why. What resources are limited? What taboos persist even when logic says they shouldn't? What happens to those who test the limits? The more your world resists its own citizens, the more your readers will believe it.

This mindset isn't about being punitive or rigid—it's about engineering resilience. When you design your world with constraints, every choice you make later, from dialogue to costume design, emerges naturally. The physics of the place do half the writing for you. That's how you achieve the holy grail of world-building: effortlessness. A reader senses that every part of your universe belongs, not because you explained it, but because it *behaves* like a system that could exist.

A Practical Workflow

Complex systems fail when they're overdesigned too early. Writers often get stuck trying to perfect their setting before testing how it behaves on the page. The better approach is iterative: **Sketch → Stress Test → Dramatize → Iterate.** You begin with a hypothesis about how your world works. Then you attempt to break it—push it to extremes, look for contradictions, imagine how different factions would exploit its vulnerabilities. Next, you dramatize the rule by writing a micro-scene: a 200-word moment that puts the rule in action through a character's perspective. Finally, you refine the rule based on what felt forced or unclear. Each loop brings your world closer to internal consistency.

To track these evolutions, keep a *World Bible*—a living document that contains not only the facts of your universe but also the reasoning behind them. Include a decision ledger: every major rule or choice should have a note explaining *why* it exists and what story functions it serves. That ledger is your defense against contradiction. When you revisit a setting years later—or build a sequel—you'll understand not just what you created but how it operates.

Another crucial part of this workflow is perspective management. Real worlds are never seen in full; every inhabitant perceives only a fragment. Apply this truth to your fiction. Use **POV filters**—decide what each group, region, or class doesn't know. The gaps between those knowledges create narrative tension and prevent over-exposition. Mystery, after all, is not withholding information; it's letting the reader sense that there's more to learn. When you track who knows what, your exposition becomes both efficient and emotionally charged. You're no longer dumping facts—you're revealing secrets through the lived experience of your characters.

Finally, embrace iteration as a creative philosophy. A world is never finished; it evolves as your story does. Rules solidify through use. If a rule fails to generate drama, change it. If it creates unexpected consequences, lean into them. The best worlds surprise even their creators.

World-building, done right, is not a detour from writing—it *is* writing. Every scene you craft is a stress test of the world's design. Every line of dialogue reflects its social architecture. Every obstacle your characters face reveals its moral physics. When all these pieces work together, story and setting become indistinguishable.

This book will teach you how to reach that level of integration— not by memorizing tropes or copying established genres, but by thinking like a systems architect. You'll learn how to design rules that hold under pressure, how to align those rules with character psychology, and how to create settings that demand stories be told about them.

Because a great world doesn't sit still on the page—it moves, grinds, and hums. It shapes meaning, tests conviction, and generates story after story. Your task, as its designer, is to set the tolerances just right and then watch the machine come alive.

Chapter 1 — World DNA: Invariants, Boundaries, and the Rule Audit

Before a writer sketches a map or names a single city, the deeper architecture of the world must be understood. Beneath every mountain range, under every empire, and even behind the metaphysical scaffolding of your magic or technology, lies the world's *DNA*—its invariants, its dials, and its tunables. These are not aesthetic choices; they are structural constants that define what is possible, probable, and forbidden within your setting. Like the laws of physics in our own universe, they govern every act of creation, every transgression, and every hope your characters pursue. Without them, your world collapses into a stage prop—fragile, arbitrary, and inert. With them, it breathes with an inner logic that readers can feel even when they can't articulate it.

1.1 Invariants, Dials, and Tunables

To design a coherent world, you must first separate your creative decisions into three categories—**invariants**, **dials**, and **tunables**. Each plays a specific role in maintaining balance and believability. The distinction among them might seem theoretical, but once you start applying it to your story's mechanics, you'll see how it liberates imagination rather than limiting it. Most failed world-building stems from confusing one for another—treating an invariant as flexible, or a dial as absolute, until the world's internal physics crumble under contradiction.

Invariants are the non-negotiables, the deep laws of your fictional universe. They define what reality itself permits. These rules must never be broken, not even by accident, or you risk rupturing the trust between your story and its reader. "No faster-than-light travel" is an invariant in a hard science fiction novel; "magic costs lifespan" is one in a grimdark fantasy. Such principles are not decorative—they impose moral and physical shape. They are the bones beneath the skin of your story.

When you define an invariant, you are defining a moral universe. For example, if you decide that magic always extracts a physical price, every spell becomes an ethical decision. Healing a child may shorten the healer's own life; resurrecting a loved one could destroy a kingdom's balance. Readers may not consciously track this rule, but they will feel the gravity of consequence behind every act. Likewise, if you declare that faster-than-light travel is impossible, exploration becomes an act of endurance rather than convenience. Empires shrink; isolation defines psychology. Characters must grapple with distance not as a plot obstacle but as a spiritual condition.

Choosing invariants is therefore a declaration of values. You're saying: "This is what this world believes in. This is what cannot be undone." Even in stories with gods, the gods themselves obey invariants. They may manipulate them, interpret them, or punish mortals who challenge them, but the rules themselves remain firm. Every convincing fictional world has these hidden constants. Tolkien's Middle-earth has mortality as its central invariant—death is unchangeable, and even divine beings are bound by it. In *Dune*, ecology is the invariant—every social, religious, and political structure exists because of planetary scarcity. Whether your world's bedrock is thermodynamics or karma, define it clearly and early.

Once your invariants are set, you can move to **dials**—the adjustable ranges within those fixed laws. Dials are what give your world its variability, tone, and sense of living change. They are the parameters that can shift, sometimes wildly, without breaking the system. Gravity might fluctuate by ten percent from region to region; literacy rates might vary from five to ninety percent; political stability could swing with each decade. Dials allow you to model inequality, transformation, and decay. They are the levers by which you evolve history.

A dial is not random; it is meaningful variation within a lawful frame. By specifying your dials, you decide where tension accumulates. A world with variable magic density, for example, creates zones of privilege and desperation. Some regions become cultural capitals of enchantment; others turn to industry or faith to compensate. A slight alteration in oxygen levels could explain the development of giant fauna in one hemisphere and delicate, short-lived species in another. Dial shifts invite adaptation—and adaptation breeds story.

Writers often overlook the narrative power of dials because they seem technical, but they are the key to dynamism. Consider literacy: in a world where only five percent of the population can read, knowledge itself becomes currency. Control of writing means control of memory, history, and truth. A rebellion led by a printer becomes not just political but existential—a fight over who has the right to remember. Raise literacy to ninety percent, and the same world becomes one of ideological chaos, where propaganda replaces ignorance and every citizen becomes an editor of reality. The rule is the same; the dial changes the story's temperature.

The third layer, **tunables**, operates closer to the narrative surface. These are world parameters tied directly to *plot beats*—settings that can be adjusted mid-story to heighten drama or reveal consequence. Tunables can shift because of character action, natural disaster, or divine intervention, but always in accordance with your established invariants and dials. Think of them as responsive systems. If the invariant says "magic costs lifespan," a tunable might define *how much* life each spell drains, and that value could increase as corruption spreads or as magical pollution builds. If your world forbids faster-than-light travel, a tunable could determine how close an experimental engine comes before catastrophic failure.

Tunables are where plot and physics intersect. They're the knobs that the story itself turns. A drought lasting three months might, through political neglect or mystical imbalance, stretch into six—pushing your society into famine and war. A social taboo might begin to weaken as generations change, creating a slow revolution of manners. Each adjustment reconfigures relationships and institutions without discarding the rules that make the world coherent.

Every time you define or alter a tunable, you must ask: *who benefits, who suffers, and what new conflicts emerge?* A rule without consequence is not a rule—it's trivia. Narrative power resides in friction. If magic suddenly becomes cheaper, who loses status? If gravity lessens by ten percent, how do architecture, warfare, and even romance adapt? People fall differently in both senses of the word. These are not thought experiments for their own sake; they are invitations to dramatize systemic change.

To ensure your design choices generate real texture, record the **implications** of every rule in your *World Bible*. For each change, list one economic, one social, and one sensory consequence. This triple lens keeps your imagination balanced. Economic consequences show how resources flow: who controls production, who is excluded, who taxes whom. Social consequences expose hierarchy: which groups rise or fall, what customs form around scarcity, what stories the culture tells to justify inequality. Sensory consequences root everything in physical experience: what does the air smell like in a world where iron corrodes instantly? How does food taste in a land of permanent twilight? What sound does currency make if it's made of glass instead of metal?

These sensory anchors transform abstract design into lived reality. They remind you that every law—no matter how conceptual—should touch the body. Readers trust worlds they can feel. When your protagonist walks through a city where gravity shifts by region, they shouldn't need exposition; their posture, their fatigue, and the way dust hangs in the air should reveal the rule. The more your system manifests through sensation, the less you need to explain.

Let's illustrate this process. Imagine you're building a post-apocalyptic archipelago where islands drift on magnetic currents. Your **invariant**: no permanent landmasses—everything moves. Your **dials**: magnetic strength and current speed vary with the seasons. Your **tunables**: communication range between islands and the reliability of navigational stones. Immediately, narrative stakes emerge. Trade depends on timing; marriages are political as much as geographic; a single storm could rearrange the known world. Now you add consequences. Economically, wealth concentrates among those who can predict drift patterns. Socially, cultures evolve nomadic rituals and myths about eternal separation. Sensory-wise, the air hums faintly with magnetic tension, compasses twitch, and the smell of ozone marks danger. Without writing a single plot, you've created a world already pregnant with stories.

The discipline of classifying rules in this way does not limit your creativity—it clarifies it. Writers often drown in their own lore because they accumulate details without hierarchy. When everything matters equally, nothing matters at all. But once you define your world's DNA—what can never change, what can flex, and what can respond to story—you acquire both structure and freedom. You can improvise confidently, knowing which boundaries you must respect and which you can bend.

Remember: the reader doesn't care how many pages of notes you've written; they care whether your world holds together under pressure. The test of a well-designed setting isn't its complexity—it's its integrity. When a single decision about resource scarcity or cultural taboo ripples naturally into economic, social, and sensory life, your world gains inevitability. It becomes not just a place where stories happen, but a place that *produces* them.

World-building begins here—not with ornament, but with architecture. Before you draw your first map, decide which rules are sacred, which are flexible, and which will tremble when your characters start to push. Everything else grows from that foundation. Constraints, after all, are not the enemy of wonder. They are its bones, the invisible skeleton that lets imagination stand upright and walk.

1.2 Boundary Conditions & Edge Cases

Every convincing world depends on its limits. Boundaries give it shape. Without them, a setting becomes a formless expanse of possibilities—an illusion of depth that collapses the moment a reader or character tests it. A boundary condition is the line between what *can* happen and what *cannot*, the edge where imagination meets physics, politics, or morality. These edges are not there to restrict the writer; they exist to generate pressure, to define what your characters must contend with or find ways around. In any functioning system—be it ecological, magical, or bureaucratic—those limits determine the direction of human ingenuity.

When you define the hard boundaries of your world, think of them as the terrain of possibility. They might be environmental, such as temperature extremes that no creature can survive, or technological, like the maximum range of communication before signal degradation. They can also be cultural—the furthest reach of law, the breaking point of faith, or the point where social custom collapses under necessity. These constraints invite the question that gives rise to story: what happens at the edge?

Mapping these limits isn't merely a logistical exercise; it's an ethical and dramatic one. Suppose your world's maximum safe flight altitude is ten thousand feet because above that, the air corrodes metals. That single rule has cascading consequences. Trade routes shrink. Warfare becomes ground-based. The myth of flight might take on religious meaning, and those who dare exceed the limit might be viewed as both pioneers and heretics. The drama lies not in the law itself but in the tension between necessity and transgression. Every story worth telling lives near a boundary, and the moment someone crosses it—knowingly or not—everything changes.

Defining boundaries also means imagining the *exploit scenarios* that naturally arise. Every rule creates an opportunity for someone to break it. This isn't cynicism; it's realism. Wherever systems exist, loopholes follow. If an empire taxes grain at harvest, smugglers will trade it by night. If a holy order restricts who may cast certain spells, secret guilds will sell them illegally. The more airtight you make a rule, the more ingenious the rebellion becomes. That friction—between authority and workaround—breathes life into your world's political and moral texture.

Exploit scenarios can be physical, like smuggling corridors that slip between jurisdictions; economic, like black-market exchanges that thrive on scarcity; or ritual, like priests who interpret doctrine to justify what's forbidden. Even in a seemingly rigid society, people find cracks in the system. These cracks are not plot holes—they're narrative veins. By exploring them, you reveal your world's adaptability and complexity. In every believable civilization, rules are not monolithic; they are contested, negotiated, and evaded.

Take, for instance, a world where sound-based magic loses potency beyond the city walls due to atmospheric interference. Such a condition immediately shapes class and geography: rural populations become second-class citizens, dependent on urban spellcasters. Yet black-market couriers might develop devices that amplify voices across the wilderness, smuggling messages or forbidden spells. This exploit doesn't contradict the rule; it confirms it by dramatizing human response. The tension between rule and loophole is the heartbeat of believable world-building.

Boundaries also serve to measure *failure thresholds*—the points where systems break down. Every rule should have a breaking point. Engines stall in dust storms, political alliances crumble under famine, magic fizzles above a certain altitude. When you know what those thresholds are, you can design stories that push toward them. Nothing builds tension like watching a world teeter near its own limits. The trick is to make failure feel inevitable, not arbitrary.

Consider a starship system that operates within a stable range of cosmic radiation. Increase exposure by even one percent, and navigation becomes impossible. The characters know the limit, fear it, and must decide whether to risk crossing it. That boundary turns scientific fact into emotional suspense. Or imagine a theocracy whose religious power depends on the appearance of miracles, yet whose rituals stop working when the population falls below a certain belief threshold. The rule's collapse becomes existential—both theological and political. Failure thresholds like these allow your world to strain, scream, and evolve.

The key is to make sure your boundaries aren't decorative—they must constrain choice. The farther a character goes toward the edge, the more meaningful their decisions become. When the law forbids travel beyond a frozen sea, a single voyage carries mythic weight. When authority cannot extend past a mountain range, exiles and outlaws find freedom but also terror. When communication cuts off after a few hundred miles, alliances fracture into misunderstanding. The reader should sense that the world pushes back, that not everything is conquerable.

Finally, boundaries help you avoid the worst sin of speculative writing: *hand-waving*. The moment a character bypasses a known rule without consequence, the reader's belief collapses. Hand-waving is the narrative equivalent of a world short-circuiting. Boundaries prevent that. If a rule is to be broken, it must cost something—time, blood, credibility, or sanity. Only then does transgression feel earned.

So, when you chart your world, mark its edges not as voids but as living frontiers. Note the altitudes where the air thins, the deserts where compasses fail, the zones where law fades into legend. Every border is an invitation to story, but only if it resists easy crossing. A strong boundary teaches both the writer and the reader what the world values—and what it fears.

1.3 The Rule Audit Template

Even the most intricate world can unravel if its rules drift quietly over time. What begins as a tight, logical system can, after a few chapters, start contradicting itself. A power that once required sacrifice becomes convenient, or a technological limit disappears because the plot demanded it. The reader may not always articulate what's wrong, but they'll feel the inconsistency. To prevent this, a writer must conduct what can be called a *rule audit*—a systematic review of how the world's mechanics function under narrative stress.

A rule audit treats each element of your world like a process with inputs, operations, and outcomes. Imagine you're not a novelist but an engineer debugging a living system. For every rule—whether it governs economics, climate, or magic—ask five questions: what are the *inputs*? what *process* transforms them? what are the *outputs*? what *costs* arise? and what *externalities*—unintended side effects—occur as a result? This model exposes weak logic before readers do.

Let's take an example. Suppose your world features "memory trading"—a form of commerce where people sell their memories for money. The *input* is human experience; the *process* is extraction through psychic or technological means; the *output* is a commodity that can be consumed by others. The *costs* might include loss of identity, trauma, or social stratification. The *externalities* could range from emotional numbing in the population to black markets that recycle false memories. By mapping the system this way, you see the chain of consequence that gives depth to your invention. Every rule, however fantastical, should pass this audit.

This method also allows you to identify collision points—moments when two subsystems of your world intersect and reveal hidden contradictions. For example, what happens when your economic system based on memory trade meets your legal system's definition of consent? Or when your planet's volatile climate disrupts long-distance communication, forcing religious institutions to adapt their hierarchies? These collisions are not bugs; they're opportunities. They create conflict and realism because they expose the friction between ideals and operations.

One powerful exercise is to write *test scenes* that stage these collisions deliberately. Don't worry about whether they fit into the main plot yet. Imagine a priest trying to enforce doctrine while dependent on a heretical technology; a merchant transporting goods across a region where physics itself grows unreliable; a soldier caught between a biological limit and an ethical command. Each test scene functions as a stress test for your world's logic. If it holds under narrative tension, it will hold for the entire story.

An audit should also include *scheduled intervals*—moments in your drafting process when you step back and re-evaluate your world's internal consistency. These might occur at the end of each major arc or act. Ask yourself: have any rules shifted unconsciously? Has convenience crept in? Are there consequences I've ignored? Writers often lose track of early constraints once momentum builds. A brief audit at key checkpoints can save you from major rewrites later.

Think of it like maintenance on a complex machine. You wouldn't run an engine indefinitely without checking its pressure and temperature. Likewise, you can't run a world through multiple storylines without verifying that its parts still align. By conducting periodic audits, you preserve the reader's trust. Every time a reader notices that a rule introduced in chapter two still governs events in chapter twelve, your world feels alive and accountable.

But rule audits are not only defensive; they're generative. Sometimes, when you examine your systems closely, you'll discover new storylines hidden within them. A cost you hadn't considered becomes a subplot. An externality turns into an entire rebellion. For instance, in a society where teleportation consumes rare minerals, an audit might reveal that mining towns are collapsing into poverty. Suddenly, you have an ecological and political subplot that enriches the main narrative. Consistency breeds complexity—not by addition, but by discovery.

There's also a psychological benefit. Performing audits trains you to think like a resident of your own world rather than its god. You begin to internalize its logic until your creative instincts align with its laws. Characters start making decisions that feel inevitable rather than scripted. The world's machinery moves beneath the story without visible gears. Readers sense this integrity even if they can't name it.

Ultimately, the rule audit is an act of respect—for your creation and for your audience. You're acknowledging that your world, however imaginary, deserves coherence. Each rule is a promise, and every promise must be kept or consciously broken with consequence.

When done thoroughly, this process transforms world-building from a collection of cool ideas into a living organism. It ensures that no element exists in isolation. A climate affects trade; trade shapes politics; politics alters faith; faith redefines art. The audit connects these systems into a single, breathing whole.

A world designed with boundaries and verified through regular audits becomes self-sustaining. Its stories emerge naturally because every mechanism leads somewhere, every limit generates a choice, and every consequence reverberates through the system. You no longer have to invent plot from scratch; you can simply watch your rules collide and evolve. That is the moment when world-building transcends description and becomes creation—when your invented world behaves like the real one, complete with error, adaptation, and grace.

Chapter 2 — Lawscaping: Physics, Metaphysics, and Cost Functions

Every world begins as a hypothesis about how reality behaves. Before it becomes a landscape, it must first become a *lawscape*—a terrain defined by cause and effect. The physical and metaphysical rules of your setting determine everything that follows: what can be built, what can be believed, how fast people can travel or communicate, and what kind of civilizations can exist at all. A writer who understands how to sculpt laws, not just describe scenery, controls the very metabolism of story. Laws are not background information; they are the invisible infrastructure of drama. Alter one, and the consequences multiply outward like concentric waves across a still lake.

To build a compelling world, you must first decide how its physics function—not merely in a scientific sense, but as a system of limitations and affordances. This is what we'll call the *physics profile* of a world: the blueprint that dictates its energy flows, motion limits, and degrees of realism. Each variable you adjust—speed, computation, gravity, thermodynamics, or even sound—reverberates across culture, economy, and myth. A believable world begins not with geography but with thresholds: how far can light travel before bending, how long can information persist before decay, how quickly can energy be exchanged without collapse?

2.1 Physics Profile

To design a world's physics profile, start not from possibility but from restraint. What can your world *not* do? In fiction, boundaries are the soil in which imagination grows. If your characters can cross continents in an hour, the politics of trade, diplomacy, and war will vanish. If instant communication exists, secrecy becomes obsolete. If energy is infinite, civilization loses friction—and story loses stakes. Every meaningful narrative depends on scarcity, and physics is the first and most universal form of scarcity.

The first category of decisions involves **speed limits**—the pace at which matter, energy, or information can move. These limits determine the size of your world's empires and the intimacy of its communities. In a world where ships crawl across vast oceans with the speed of wind, news becomes rumor and history overtakes memory. Authority weakens with distance; independence thrives at the periphery. Conversely, if your world allows instantaneous travel or communication, the map shrinks until every conflict becomes internal—social, ideological, or psychological rather than geographical. Decide early whether your world moves at the tempo of the horse, the telegraph, or the photon, because everything else will align around that rhythm.

Movement speed shapes narrative tension. In a slow world, journeys define character. In a fast one, immediacy defines morality—every decision echoes instantly across systems. But speed also shapes *meaning*. A story set in a slow-moving world must honor patience, endurance, and isolation; one set in a hyper-fast realm must grapple with overload and entropy. Think of speed not as a technical feature but as a cultural metaphor.

Next comes **energy density**—how much usable energy exists per unit of effort. This single choice underwrites technology, warfare, ecology, and even theology. Low energy worlds breed humility and craft: firewood economies, windships, and community rituals built around labor. High energy worlds breed ambition and acceleration: jetcraft, planetary industry, and an appetite for conquest. The higher the energy gradient, the faster civilization transforms. Yet high energy also breeds fragility. A society that relies on concentrated power—be it nuclear, magical, or divine—teeters perpetually on the edge of catastrophe. Decide not just how much energy exists but how stable it is. Does it leak, fade, corrupt, or explode? Does harnessing it require skill, sacrifice, or faith? Energy isn't only what keeps worlds alive; it's what keeps them honest.

Then there is **information friction**—the resistance that slows or distorts the flow of knowledge. This may seem abstract, but it's one of the most powerful storytelling levers available. A high-friction world—where news travels slowly, archives decay, and memory is unreliable—creates cultures of rumor and myth. Power concentrates in scribes, priests, or data-keepers who control the written or spoken word. A low-friction world—where data travels flawlessly and instantly—creates surveillance states, transparency cults, or collective intelligences that struggle to preserve individuality. The world's information climate defines how people trust one another, how they lie, and what they fear losing.

Imagine a civilization where radio signals degrade unpredictably, scattering messages into ghostly echoes that overlap with older transmissions. The result might be a world obsessed with divination and repetition, where people treat static as prophecy and historians double as interpreters of interference. Or picture a planet where all speech above a certain altitude turns to silence, forcing settlements into valleys and shaping a theology around the sacred quiet of the peaks. Every physical quirk becomes a cultural law.

A well-defined physics profile also depends on your chosen **granularity of realism**. Not every aspect of your world must obey hard logic. The key is to decide *where* realism should be precise and where it can blur for stylistic or thematic effect. You might choose hard orbital mechanics but soft acoustics, precise economics but impressionistic biology. The balance should serve the story's tone. A gritty survival narrative demands firm physical laws, while a mythic allegory thrives on suggestion and dream logic. The problem arises only when the boundaries between "hard" and "soft" shift without reason. Readers will accept implausibility as long as it is *consistent*.

Granularity is not about how many equations you include but how predictable your world feels. Hard realism delivers satisfaction through causality: readers enjoy watching every action obey its consequences. Soft realism delivers satisfaction through resonance: readers accept mystery as long as it feels emotionally coherent. The skill lies in blending the two without contradiction. A world can be both rational and poetic, as long as its internal rhythm remains stable.

No physics profile is complete without **environmental asymmetries**—the natural imbalances that create diversity and narrative opportunity. Perfect equilibrium is sterile. Worlds come alive when they tilt—when day lasts longer than night, when magnetic storms warp navigation, when one hemisphere drowns in monsoon while the other bakes in drought. These asymmetries force adaptation and specialization. They produce regions with distinct identities, economies, and mythologies.

Think of the Sahara and the Nile, the Himalayas and the plains, or in fiction, Arrakis and Caladan. Contrast is the mother of culture. A world of constant temperature would have no seasons and therefore no metaphors for renewal or decay. A world with unstable magnetic fields might produce nomads who navigate by sound instead of sight. A planet locked in tidal rotation could split its civilizations between the eternal day of the facing side and the perpetual night of the far one—each side imagining the other as heaven or hell. Such asymmetries do more than enrich setting; they shape consciousness.

When designing these environmental conditions, look for points of collision. What happens at the twilight zones—the borders between hot and cold, light and shadow, silence and sound? Frontier zones are narrative goldmines because they embody transition. They are the physical analogs of character arcs. Inhabitants who live at those thresholds must negotiate identity daily, torn between opposing truths. Worlds that contain such gradients feel alive because they mirror the human condition: constant adjustment to uneven circumstances.

Your physics profile, then, is not a collection of numbers or trivia—it's the emotional architecture of the world. Every law you set down carries a tone. A low-gravity planet will produce not only different architecture but a different sense of grace and risk. A society that depends on unstable energy sources will develop rituals of caution, fatalism, or defiance. The physics shape the psychology.

To construct a convincing lawscape, begin small. Define three constants: a speed limit, an energy density, and an information friction. Watch how they interact. If travel is slow, communication must compensate, or isolation defines culture. If energy is scarce, ingenuity replaces brute force. If information is abundant, secrecy becomes a luxury. Every adjustment propagates through every layer of life, creating what might be called a *cascade of consequences.* The physics profile is not the end of world-building; it is its ignition key.

As you continue refining your world, remember that the physical laws are not fixed by science but by *story purpose.* Your physics must serve theme. If your narrative explores power and restraint, make energy scarce. If it examines faith and uncertainty, introduce phenomena that defy measurement. If it confronts memory and loss, let information degrade or mutate over time. The physical world becomes a metaphorical mirror of the inner one.

The art of world-building, at its highest level, lies in understanding how matter and meaning co-evolve. When a reader feels that a planet's gravity or a spell's cost reflects the moral weight of the story, immersion deepens into belief. The laws of your world are not only technical—they are ethical, psychological, and poetic. They teach the reader what the universe itself believes about balance and consequence.

To change one law is to rewrite destiny. That is why the physics profile must be deliberate. Once you alter the behavior of heat, time, or sound, you've rewritten everything built upon them—religion, economy, architecture, and desire. Your task is not to manage those ripples but to *count* them, one by one, until the pattern becomes inevitable. Only then will your world feel not invented but discovered.

2.2 Magic/Tech as Protocols with Prices

In most stories, whether the setting leans toward fantasy or science fiction, a world's sense of wonder rests upon its extraordinary systems—the mechanisms through which humans manipulate forces larger than themselves. Call it magic, call it technology, or call it divine interference: it functions as a *protocol*, a set of permissions and verifications that determines who can act, under what conditions, and at what cost. The difference between a believable system of power and an arbitrary one lies in how rigorously you treat it as a rule-governed process rather than a limitless convenience.

Magic and technology both serve as expressions of control. They transform intent into outcome. But unlike omnipotence, control must be *earned*. A well-designed world ensures that every exercise of power is conditional—anchored to prerequisites, authenticated by ritual, lineage, or expertise. In the same way a programmer must compile code within syntactic limits, or a scientist must replicate experiments under defined variables, the world's manipulators—mages, engineers, shamans, or technocrats—must operate within their protocol's logic. This approach replaces the vague mysticism of "because magic" with the rigor of "because system."

The first question is always *who can invoke the protocol?* Access defines hierarchy. If the ability to shape fire is reserved for those born under an eclipse, society will organize around those few. If neural implants grant computational advantage but require invasive surgery, class and courage become intertwined. If spellcasting demands fluency in a dead language, education itself becomes a gatekeeper of power. The act of authentication—whether by oath, bloodline, credential, or gene sequence—creates narrative texture and moral complexity. A world where anyone can access the extraordinary is egalitarian but volatile; one where power is rare is stable but unjust. Choose your imbalance carefully.

Then comes the question of *what prerequisites* exist. A world where technology depends on ambient energy may suffer rolling blackouts that freeze whole economies. A magical society that requires rare reagents might collapse when an ecological disaster eradicates a key plant. Preconditions aren't decorative—they tether your power system to geography and history. If certain ores or sacred waters are needed to perform essential functions, wars will erupt over their control. Prerequisites transform abstract abilities into tangible economies.

A powerful world feels *expensive*. Every manipulation of nature should cost something measurable—energy, effort, time, sanity, or ecological stability. This is where the concept of **cost curves** enters: the more intense or wide-reaching the act, the steeper the price. The smallest incantations might cost a few heartbeats or a pinch of iron, while continent-shifting spells might drain lifespans or trigger famines. In a technological world, the same principle holds: higher power consumption generates exponentially higher risk, pollution, or moral compromise. A system without cost becomes a narrative dead end; a system with escalating prices creates tension, strategy, and restraint.

Costs don't have to be purely physical. Psychological and spiritual debts can be just as potent. Memory loss as a side effect of spellcasting forces mages to weigh progress against identity. A cybernetic engineer who sacrifices empathy for processing speed embodies the same equation. These internalized costs mirror the outer ones and allow readers to feel the gravity of choice. The audience must sense that every act of creation subtracts something from the world or the self.

Yet cost alone isn't enough. Power must also be *risky*. To make a system feel alive, build in **operational hazards**—the possibility that the protocol misfires, backfires, or becomes unstable under pressure. A spell might succeed but twist its intent, interpreting commands too literally, like a machine obeying flawed code. A technological weapon might overheat, melt, or leak radiation. The point is not to punish characters arbitrarily, but to remind them—and the reader—that mastery always rides alongside uncertainty. Perfect reliability kills suspense.

These hazards also serve as story generators. A single malfunction can spark a whole plot: a city's communication grid collapses because a solar storm interferes with its data architecture; a ritual goes wrong because the caster's lineage isn't pure enough; a swarm of autonomous drones evolves its own defensive instincts. By designing protocols with built-in vulnerabilities, you give yourself endless narrative tools. Each malfunction exposes the limits of knowledge and the hubris of those who think they can bypass the rules of their own creation.

Consider how such a protocol shapes culture. If magic requires spoken formulas, then stuttering or silence becomes a disability with social weight. If energy systems rely on vocal harmonics, choirs become political institutions. If divine power answers only those who perform precise moral acts, religion and governance merge into the same body. The details of invocation—how, when, and by whom—turn metaphysics into sociology.

A key feature of believable systems is **friction**—the obstacles between intent and execution. When power requires procedure, it slows the pace of miracles. Every step in a protocol becomes an opportunity for human error or moral questioning. A knight who must swear an oath before activating her blade might hesitate at the crucial moment. A scientist who must calibrate his machine for hours before ignition feels the weight of responsibility. Friction humanizes the extraordinary, grounding spectacle in process.

Ultimately, magic or technology must behave like a language— a grammar of possibility with rules, exceptions, and idioms. Once you think of your system as linguistic, consistency becomes easier. Every spell or device is a sentence written within that grammar. Errors produce distortion, and distortion produces drama. The beauty of this approach is that it allows infinite creativity within a coherent frame. You can invent new effects without contradicting the old ones, as long as they obey syntax.

What makes such systems memorable is not their scale but their moral dimension. Power, once mechanized, invites questions of ethics. Who decides the acceptable level of risk? Who pays for the environmental fallout of a spell that heals by draining surrounding life? When technology becomes indistinguishable from divine power, who gets to regulate its use? The answers shape not only storylines but philosophies. Your system of rules becomes your world's theology—the invisible contract between mortals and the forces they wield.

The difference between spectacle and meaning lies here. A lightning bolt is spectacle. The knowledge that it cost someone a decade of memories—that's meaning.

2.3 Paradoxes & Failure Modes

No world can sustain perfection for long. The moment you introduce complex systems—magical, technological, or political—they begin to fail. The art of *lawscaping* is not to prevent these failures but to anticipate them, to design a structure resilient enough to break beautifully. A world without paradox is a world without drama. The key is to prepare for the moments when your own rules collide, overlap, or collapse under contradiction.

Failure modes arise wherever two laws intersect and produce outcomes that neither system alone can manage. These collisions give texture to reality, because real worlds are messy. When healing magic meets a mutating plague, does the spell adapt, or does it amplify the infection? When teleportation exists, how does property law define theft? If artificial intelligences can predict crime, what happens to the concept of justice? Each paradox exposes the moral fault lines beneath your world's logic.

The worst kind of world-breaking happens when an author improvises solutions to these contradictions mid-story. Readers feel it immediately: the sudden appearance of a "null field" or a "rare mineral" that disables magic reads as an excuse, not a design. To avoid this, **pre-write your exception handling.** Establish the conditions under which your systems fail before you need them to. These failures should make sense within the world's internal physics. A silence zone where sound-based spells die might result from natural geological resonance. A null field that disables technology could be the side effect of cosmic radiation. The important thing is that exceptions feel like *discoveries*, not inventions made to rescue the plot.

Paradoxes are not mistakes—they are the crucibles of narrative meaning. They test whether your world behaves like a living system that can adapt to stress. A world immune to paradox becomes sterile; one full of contradictions without explanation collapses into chaos. The sweet spot is controlled instability: a reality that flexes, cracks, and reforms according to its own principles.

Beyond the metaphysical, every society that lives with unpredictable power must evolve a **containment culture**—a network of precautions, institutions, and rituals built to manage risk. This is one of the richest veins of world texture you can mine. Where there is danger, there will be procedure. Where there is potential misuse, there will be courts, guilds, and audits. A civilization that treats power lightly feels fake; one that ritualizes it feels lived-in.

Imagine an academy that licenses spellcasters the way modern societies license pilots or doctors, with inspections, psychological evaluations, and ethical codes. Picture a world where anti-tech cults protest neural enhancement labs, citing ancient prophecies about the loss of soul. Or consider a bureaucracy that taxes every teleportation jump to account for the environmental damage of energy distortion. These institutions make your extraordinary believable because they show the mundane scaffolding required to contain it.

Containment culture also humanizes the fantastic. Safety gear becomes a symbol of humility: goggles enchanted against psychic glare, gloves designed to prevent accidental summoning, or wards that suppress emotion during rituals. Every precaution tells a story about prior catastrophe. People don't invent regulation without having suffered first. By embedding such

details, you suggest a long history of trial, error, and adaptation—
the hallmark of realism.

Tracking **law collisions** is another way to ensure internal
consistency. Think of your world's systems as overlapping
circles: political law, natural law, magical law, technological law,
moral law. Where they intersect, sparks fly. The priest-scientist
who must choose between doctrine and data embodies this
tension. So does the mage forced to testify in a secular court about
a phenomenon that defies measurement. Each intersection
produces ethical ambiguity, and ethical ambiguity is the soil of
drama.

Failure modes also remind us that every invention is a form of
hubris. The moment humans—or any sentient species—believe
they can dominate nature or the divine, the system pushes back.
The collapse of overused magic fields, the rebellion of self-aware
machines, the spiritual corruption of overreaching priests—these
are not clichés if they emerge from your world's logic. They are
the feedback loops of creation itself, the moral physics of
consequence.

The final test of your lawscape is whether it *contains* its
paradoxes without erasing them. A believable world doesn't
eliminate contradiction; it manages it through culture, myth, and
procedure. When citizens learn to live with instability, you know
your world is mature. A society that holds festivals to honor the
failure of spells, or that builds shrines around malfunctioning
relics, feels more alive than one that pretends perfection is
possible.

In the end, paradox is not the enemy of coherence—it is its proof.
The moment your laws begin to strain against each other, your
world stops being a schematic and becomes a living ecosystem.
Every rule that can fail, every system that must be audited, every
institution that tries and sometimes fails to control power—all of

these details converge into a sense of realism deeper than description.

By embracing paradox and planning for failure, you create not a brittle utopia but a resilient universe. Readers don't fall in love with perfection; they fall in love with tension, repair, and endurance. The cracks in your world are where the light of meaning gets in.

Chapter 3 — Terrain, Climate, and Deep Time

Every world begins with the ground beneath its characters' feet. Before kingdoms rise or languages form, before myths are told or stars are charted, there is geology—the slow and relentless sculptor of fate. Terrain is not backdrop; it is destiny cast in stone. Mountains determine where people stop migrating, rivers dictate where they trade, deserts decide who hungers and who conquers. When you trace the lineage of any civilization, you find that its moral codes and political hierarchies descend directly from the shape of its land. Geography is the first law, and deep time is the silent author that wrote it.

3.1 Geologic Backstory

Creating the geologic backstory of a fictional world is not merely an exercise in mapmaking—it is the act of writing prehistory. To design convincing terrain, you must think like both an archaeologist and a mythographer. Your task is to weave natural process and human meaning into a single continuum, where every mountain and basin tells a story of pressure, erosion, eruption, and endurance. Whether your world obeys plate tectonics or some fantasy equivalent—a breathing earth, a cosmic serpent, a sentient crust—the logic must feel consistent and traceable. Readers may not consciously analyze why a continent's coastline curves a certain way, but they will feel its authenticity when the land behaves as though it has lived for eons before the first character was born.

The first step is to establish **tectonic logic**, even if you rename or reimagine it. In our own world, continents drift, collide, and fracture. Oceans open like wounds and heal into mountains. That same rhythm—expansion, compression, and subduction—can underpin any believable planet or plane. Decide where your world's restless energy concentrates. Are there fault lines where magic bleeds through the crust, or fractures where divine wars once shattered the mantle? Do your continents grind against each other, producing volcanic chains rich in obsidian and myth? Even if your setting is purely fantastical, giving it a geological metabolism—motion over time—makes it breathe.

Tectonic structure explains more than shape; it determines destiny. A land ringed by mountains may evolve in isolation, its culture inward-looking, self-protective, and spiritually tied to stone. A wide, unbroken plain invites expansion, pastoralism, and empire. An archipelago breeds seafarers who value navigation, exchange, and mythic fluidity. Terrain dictates temperament. When you define your world's tectonic skeleton, you are defining the emotional geometry of its people.

Geologic time moves in cataclysms and slow grace. Glaciations advance like patient sculptors, carving valleys that will cradle future cities. Meteoric impacts gouge out inland seas that later host civilizations drawn to their mineral wealth. Extinct volcanoes become pilgrimage sites, their craters filled with sacred lakes. Each ancient disaster becomes a mythic scar, carried in the stories of survivors and descendants. When you embed such deep-time events into your setting, you anchor its mythos in material history. Gods and heroes may claim credit for shaping the land, but the bedrock tells a different tale—one of pressure and persistence.

Consider the emotional power of a landscape that remembers. A desert might once have been an ocean, its sand whispering with the ghosts of fish. A mountain range might conceal fossils of trees from an age before men or elves, turning every quarry into a revelation. These details remind readers that civilizations are young compared to the bones of their world. The land itself becomes an elder character, patient and unsentimental, observing the rise and fall of those who presume to own it.

When you design a geologic backstory, connect **resource seams** to the rhythms of settlement and conflict. Where there is salt, there is civilization; where there is gold, there is greed. Mineral distribution is not decorative—it is geopolitical DNA. Cities rise where the land offers advantage: fresh water, fertile soil, defensible cliffs, or tradeable resources. Wars ignite where two veins intersect—a mountain full of copper beside a valley full of coal, a river delta rich in alluvium beside a desert dotted with oil. Even in worlds ruled by magic, scarcity and access remain the primary engines of history. The richest fantasy settings honor that realism by tying wonder to geography.

For instance, if your world's energy source is aether drawn from crystalline seams deep within fault lines, then mining becomes both sacred and perilous. Entire cultures might build their identity around proximity to these veins, while others become dependent on their exports. Over centuries, trade routes follow those seams like arteries, and wars scar them like infections. The physical distribution of resource equals the moral distribution of power.

Geology also influences migration and belief. Rivers carved by ancient glaciers may become pilgrimage routes long after their economic importance fades. A mountain range that once erupted could become the axis of a creation myth—the place where gods first breathed life into ash. Inhabitants who live near tectonic faults may see earthquakes not as disasters but as divine communications, the planet's voice breaking through stone. Every tremor reinforces a worldview: that the earth is alive, that instability is natural, that permanence is illusion. When you align natural history with spiritual meaning, the result feels organic, inevitable, and profound.

Think about how terrain changes through *time*, not just space. Continents drift; coasts erode; lakes evaporate. The map of your world one thousand years ago should differ from the one your characters use now. Perhaps ancient roads lead to dry seaports or submerged temples. Fossilized forests lie beneath modern deserts, proof that climate and fortune shift together. The more you allow geological change to ripple through cultural memory, the more your world gains credibility. Myths of lost continents or drowned kingdoms become plausible when the land itself is restless.

A world's deep-time events should also leave **economic and emotional residue**. A glaciation might expose salt beds that sustain trade millennia later. A meteor impact could scatter rare metals that spark industrial revolutions or magical booms. Conversely, an ancient catastrophe might poison the soil, creating forbidden zones rich in superstition. Every scar of the past has aftershocks in the present. The ruins of collapsed civilizations buried under volcanic ash become archaeological treasures—or taboos. The survivors' descendants may turn their ancestors' failure into ritual humility or imperial warning. Deep time is not just a setting—it is memory encoded in landscape.

Geology, at its core, is narrative structure stretched over eons. Pressure builds, eruption releases, sediment accumulates—these are not just physical processes but story rhythms. Worlds that ignore this tempo feel weightless. But when you let your terrain record trauma and recovery, the setting begins to carry subtext. A collapsed mountain range speaks of hubris punished. A gorge carved by ancient floods becomes a metaphor for persistence. A coastline riddled with fossils reminds every inhabitant that life is transient but continuous.

If you treat land as static, your story loses tension. But when land becomes active—shifting, decaying, healing—it mirrors the arc of civilization itself. People migrate because rivers change course. Empires fall because volcanoes choke trade routes. Religions form because the ground rumbles in patterns mistaken for divine rhythm. The land teaches adaptation, and through adaptation, culture evolves.

Geology also offers a unique opportunity for symbolic storytelling. A mountain may be more than a rock formation—it can represent hierarchy, aspiration, or isolation. A river embodies time and continuity; a desert, silence and trial. By tracing these symbols back to their geological origins, you keep them from feeling arbitrary. If your world's greatest mountain once rose from a magical collision of worlds, its sacredness will feel earned. If your desert was born of divine punishment—oceans boiled away during an ancient war—its desolation will carry both myth and science.

Lastly, remember that deep time humbles every inhabitant. No matter how advanced their technology or powerful their sorcery, they live on borrowed ground. The mountains will outlast them. The rivers will rewrite their borders. The tectonic pulse of the planet will continue long after their names have faded into dust. When you convey that awareness—when your characters feel small before the scale of the earth—you achieve something rare in world-building: awe without exposition.

A well-crafted geologic backstory reminds readers that history did not begin with human memory. The world has its own biography, written in stone and erosion, explosion and sediment. Every cliff is a page, every fossil a footnote. When you understand that the land is not scenery but scripture, you will stop inventing terrain and start *uncovering* it. And in doing so, you will give your readers the same sensation that great explorers feel when they crest a ridge and see, for the first time, a valley that has waited a million years for a witness.

3.2 Climate Cells & Microclimates

If geology writes the bones of a world, climate gives it breath. The way air moves, the way rain falls, and the way heat settles into valleys or escapes across oceans—all of it defines the rhythm of daily life. You can trace the shape of civilizations through the sky as easily as through the soil. Wind patterns decide trade routes; currents dictate contact between continents; and temperature gradients carve boundaries far stronger than any wall or border. A convincing climate is not decoration—it's the invisible hand that shapes culture, economy, architecture, and even thought.

To make a world feel alive, you must think like the weather itself. Start with motion: how does the air circulate? Prevailing winds are the conveyor belts of culture, carrying both pollen and rumor. In one hemisphere, trade winds might funnel ships and caravans along predictable seasonal corridors; in another, chaotic gusts could isolate entire coastlines for months. When the air stagnates, plagues linger. When it races, empires expand. The direction and consistency of those winds matter far more than the temperature on any given day.

Then there are the oceans, the great moderators. Currents are planetary arteries transferring warmth and possibility. A warm current can turn an otherwise frozen shore into a lush agricultural paradise, while a cold one can strip the vitality from a coastline that should, by latitude, be blooming. Where currents meet, fogs form—dense, ghostlike barriers that hide ships or myths. Entire maritime religions can spring up around those liminal zones, worshipping the gray veil where sea and sky dissolve.

Rain and its absence govern destiny more ruthlessly than kings. Where mountains rise, they intercept moisture, wringing clouds dry on one side and casting the far slope into parched shadow. These *rain shadows* create dramatic juxtapositions: lush kingdoms facing barren wastelands, civilizations of plenty separated from nomads of necessity by a single ridge. Such boundaries generate both envy and trade, pilgrimage and plunder. In a well-designed world, a single mountain range might explain centuries of war, a recurring monsoon, or an entire theology of water.

Fog belts, hurricane alleys, drought corridors—each of these is a kind of narrative infrastructure. If hurricanes predictably strike one coast every six years, the architecture there must adapt, with stilt houses, reinforced docks, and folklore built around the return of "storm season." Conversely, a city perpetually shrouded in fog becomes a place of secrecy, introspection, or melancholy. Writers often treat weather as mood; in reality, it's memory. People build their identities around what the sky has always done to them.

The finer texture of a believable world comes from **microclimates**—the small, hyperlocal quirks of temperature, humidity, and light that differentiate one valley from the next, or even one street from another. A capital city might sit at the junction of three microclimates: a humid riverfront that breeds fishmongers and superstition, an elevated district cooled by evening breezes where scholars and nobles cluster, and a crowded industrial quarter that radiates heat long after sunset. Over centuries, these thermal differences become social ones. Accent, cuisine, and temperament shift with altitude and exposure.

In the countryside, microclimates carve dialects and economies. A single valley may produce a distinctive wine because the sun strikes it at a slightly different angle, or because the fog lifts an hour later than in neighboring regions. Shepherds grazing flocks on the cooler north-facing slopes develop different songs and stories than farmers tilling the southern terraces. Even animals evolve to match their microhabitats, reinforcing the illusion of natural inevitability. When readers sense this quiet specificity—the way weather changes with the bend of a road—they believe in the world without needing maps.

Cities, too, have their weather. The *urban heat island* effect turns dense districts into cauldrons, altering everything from health to politics. The poor live where the air stagnates; the powerful build gardens where wind can find them. Chimney smoke, alchemical exhaust, or floating bio-reactors might thicken the air until the city itself becomes semi-sentient—a creature exhaling its own atmosphere. Imagine the way smell and light differ from district to district: copper tangs near the foundries, ozone in the mage quarter, fermenting fruit where market refuse decomposes in tropical damp. These differences create not just setting but social texture.

Climate, of course, governs time. The pulse of a year—the swing from abundance to scarcity—dictates calendars, rituals, and emotional tone. The wet season might bring both fertility and fever; the dry season, both hunger and spiritual reflection. In agrarian worlds, harvest festivals aren't arbitrary—they are moral events that reaffirm gratitude and hierarchy. Even industrial or interstellar societies feel the echo of seasonality: shipping lanes open when storms recede, power grids strain during heatwaves, markets rise and fall with weather forecasts. When you make readers *feel* the calendar through shortage, scent, and light, the illusion of reality deepens.

Climate also shapes language itself. In deserts, people speak in terms of shade and direction; in tundras, vocabulary blooms around snow, ice, and endurance. Idioms evolve from weather. A culture battered by monsoons may use "to reef the sails" as a metaphor for humility. A mountain society might use the phrase "above the fog" to mean clarity or moral vision. When climate infiltrates speech, it ceases to be setting and becomes worldview.

To design convincing climates, you don't need meteorological precision—you need emotional accuracy. Ask how it feels to live where wind never stops, or where dawn takes two hours to arrive, or where rain falls sideways for weeks. What kind of patience or fatalism does that breed? What gestures—turning faces from grit, bowing under snow—become part of daily choreography? The weather teaches posture long before it teaches science.

3.3 Disasters & Slow Variables

If climate is the heartbeat of a world, disasters are its arrhythmias—the sudden shocks that remind inhabitants of their fragility. Yet beyond the spectacular lies the slow erosion, the creeping variables that change civilizations one grain at a time. Together, these forces—both abrupt and glacial—form the long tension between humanity and the planet that carries it. Writers who ignore these dynamics risk creating worlds that feel static. Real worlds, even imaginary ones, must *move*, must threaten, must decay.

Recurring hazards give a setting its rhythm. A monsoon that fails every fifth year becomes a grim drumbeat in collective memory. Families plan weddings and harvests around the odds of catastrophe. A volcanic ashfall that darkens skies every century reshapes religion: people worship cycles of destruction as divine renewal. The repetition of disaster breeds ritual, bureaucracy, and resilience. When readers encounter a culture that knows how to *wait* for the storm—stockpiling grain, retelling cautionary myths, performing appeasement rites—they sense the continuity of generations.

The best catastrophes aren't surprises; they are appointments kept by nature. A hurricane season that "always comes early" this year can still feel momentous precisely because everyone knew it would come *sometime.* Anticipation, not shock, drives the narrative realism of disaster. You can measure a society's maturity by how it organizes its fear—whether through superstition, engineering, or fatalism.

Alongside the dramatic hazards are the **slow variables**—the invisible shifts that unravel worlds from within. Soil fertility, aquifer depletion, forest loss, silt choking river deltas—these slow-motion disasters define dynastic arcs better than any war. Empires fall not because of invasion but because irrigation canals clog with salt, or forests shrink until shipbuilding ceases. These changes are the real measure of time, the heartbeat of deep history. When you build them into your setting, you give it a memory longer than any character's lifespan.

Imagine a kingdom whose prosperity depends on fertile volcanic soil. For centuries, they over-farm it, and the yield declines so gradually that no one notices until famine becomes normal. Or picture a desert empire that draws water from ancient aquifers, the level dropping imperceptibly each decade. By the time the wells fail, the capital's wealth is built on a vanishing foundation. These are not sudden tragedies—they are elegies for civilizations that mistook the future for an endless extension of the present.

Tracking slow variables also allows you to model generational storytelling. Grandparents recall rivers that no longer exist; children grow up thinking drought is natural. Myths evolve to justify loss. A vanished forest becomes the home of forgotten gods; a dried sea becomes the stage for pilgrimage. Over centuries, what begins as ecological decline transforms into theology and politics. When your world carries these sedimentary layers of meaning, readers feel its age in their bones.

Every society living under risk develops what might be called a **risk culture**—a pattern of behavior, superstition, and governance born from coexistence with danger. In floodplains, people build on stilts and hold annual ceremonies of appeasement; in earthquake zones, they construct shrines that double as shelters. In more advanced or cynical societies, insurance guilds and risk brokers rise to power, quietly influencing politics through the arithmetic of disaster. A levee becomes not just an engineering project but a metaphor for faith in control, and the fight to fund it becomes the story of corruption and class.

Risk cultures reveal how a world interprets vulnerability. Some societies turn it into religion, others into bureaucracy. A theocracy might claim each drought as divine punishment, while a merchant republic measures risk in premiums and interest rates. Even seemingly primitive customs—such as sacred groves left untouched in flood zones—can embody sophisticated environmental wisdom. These "ritual protections" become the ancestors of zoning laws and conservation ethics. When you embed them, you show that your world has learned from pain.

Disasters also have social consequences. They redistribute power and wealth, exposing who profits from catastrophe. After a famine, grain merchants rise; after a flood, engineers become heroes. A culture repeatedly struck by the same hazard develops a collective personality: fatalistic, stoic, ingenious, or suspicious of outsiders. Inhabitants of earthquake regions may prize adaptability; those of drought zones may idolize foresight. Disaster molds character as surely as it molds terrain.

It's easy to think of catastrophe only as destruction, but in narrative terms it's also revelation. When the flood comes, the architecture of society is laid bare: who can swim, who hoards boats, who gets left behind. The physical event strips away illusion. A volcano or typhoon becomes a kind of moral audit, exposing both the resilience and the hypocrisy of those in power. These moments, when nature asserts itself, remind readers that the world is not neutral—it has temperament and will.

Yet the subtler power belongs to the slow variables. A city rebuilt after a fire might stand taller, prouder, but if its harbor continues to silt up year after year, its decline is inevitable. Such long decay offers a different kind of drama: not the spectacle of collapse, but the ache of inevitability. A merchant's diary noting that ships take longer to reach the sea each decade tells a more haunting story than a single day of ruin.

In the end, both disaster and gradual change teach the same lesson: worlds, like people, are mortal. They erode, adjust, remember. When you build these dynamics into your setting, you allow time to become a living force, shaping not just history but identity. The survivors of one generation become the cautionary tales of the next. Cities adapt, fail, and are reborn under new names, but the river keeps changing course.

By designing climates that breathe and catastrophes that return, by giving your world both cycles and scars, you grant it that rarest of qualities—continuity. Readers will feel that long before they analyze it. The land, the weather, the disaster, and the culture—together they form a single sentence written by time, rewritten by endurance.

Chapter 4 — Ecologies, Food Webs, and Disease

Civilization is built not on stone, nor on law, but on energy. Every city, empire, and army exists only as long as the world beneath it can sustain hunger—human, animal, mechanical, or magical. The moment the flow of energy falters, kingdoms crumble, species vanish, gods grow silent. Ecology is not scenery; it is the metabolism of existence. To design a living world, you must begin not with its rulers or heroes, but with its food chain—with the green pulse of what feeds what. The architecture of life defines the architecture of story.

4.1 Energy & Trophic Architecture

A believable ecology begins with the question: *Where does the energy come from?* Everything that moves, breathes, or thinks in your world depends on that answer. The sun, whether literal or metaphorical, is the origin of all consequence. In some worlds, it's a blazing star whose strength dictates the fertility of fields and the rhythms of migration. In others, it may be a wan, fading orb whose dimness compresses life into narrow belts of habitability. And in some, energy comes from stranger sources: phosphorescent fungi, magical currents, titanic beasts whose bodies radiate warmth like moving suns. Whatever its form, your world's primary productivity—its baseline capacity to turn raw energy into food—defines its scale of possibility.

In a lush, high-energy world, ecosystems can support dense populations and vast armies. Cities spread like moss, and wars are fought not for survival but for ideology. In a low-energy world—one orbiting a dim star or trapped under perpetual ash—

life becomes sparse, specialized, and fragile. Armies shrink to raiding bands. Economies revolve around scarcity, and spiritual traditions praise conservation as holiness. Energy is the first and final constraint of all politics.

The concept of *trophic architecture*—the structure of who eats whom—applies to every layer of creation, not just biology. Farmers and hunters depend on how energy flows through the land. Priests and merchants depend on how it flows through faith and trade. Even a system of magic has its trophic levels: sources, conduits, consumers, and scavengers. By tracing those flows, you discover not only ecology but sociology.

Start at the bottom: the primary producers. In our world, these are plants and algae—organisms that turn light into life. In yours, they might be luminous reefs of magical coral, airborne spore clouds drifting through the stratosphere, or subterranean mats of fungi feeding on geothermal heat. Whatever form they take, they must be abundant, renewable, and vulnerable. The fate of civilizations depends on them, even if no one notices. When you design your producers, you are setting the heartbeat of your world's economy. A single shift in their abundance—a blight, a season of darkness, a divine curse—can collapse empires faster than any sword.

Above them climb the consumers, predators, and scavengers, each layer more energy-hungry than the last. The higher the predator, the rarer it must be. This rule applies to both ecosystems and civilizations. Predatory species require large territories; predatory nations require vast resources. A society of conquerors must rely on fertile subjects just as a lion depends on herds. When you respect this equilibrium, your world gains realism: no empire can devour endlessly without starving itself.

Then come the **keystone species**—those creatures whose presence sustains entire ecosystems, whose decline triggers collapse. In your world, a keystone might be an insect that pollinates sacred crops, or a leviathan whose migrations stir nutrient-rich currents. Perhaps it's a mundane herbivore whose hides provide both armor and roof tiles. When these species falter, cultures change. Architecture adapts, clothing evolves, weaponry shifts. If the world once relied on giant beasts for transport and they vanish, roads crumble and cities retract inward. If a magical pollinator dies off, famine becomes not only physical but spiritual, as rituals lose meaning. The death of one species becomes the death of an era.

The beauty of designing keystone species lies in watching their influence ripple through unexpected domains. A creature hunted to near extinction might once have provided bone for flutes and sinew for bowstrings, shaping music and warfare alike. When it disappears, new materials—and new aesthetics—must arise. People's songs grow softer; their weapons change form. In this way, biology becomes anthropology.

Waste, too, is destiny. Every functioning ecology must recycle its dead, and so must every civilization. What a culture does with its refuse reveals more about its beliefs than any scripture. Waste is a mirror of hierarchy. The rich conceal it; the poor live among it; the sacred transform it. In agrarian societies, composting is both necessity and philosophy—the transformation of decay into renewal. In urban or industrial ones, waste becomes class warfare: who breathes the smoke, who drinks the runoff, who profits from the cleanup.

When you design your world's *waste loops*, you design its conscience. Do people feed scraps to sacred animals, turning refuse into ritual? Do they ship garbage to colonies, outsourcing guilt along trade winds? Does a magical residue build up in the soil, poisoning the crops that feed the poor first? In fantasy worlds, waste often becomes literal corruption—magical entropy that seeps into rivers, creating monsters. In science fiction, it becomes pollution of data or memory, the byproduct of minds running too hot. In both, it is the measure of sustainability.

Even taboo plays a role in the waste economy. Every culture has substances considered unclean, forbidden, or dangerous. These taboos may be practical—preventing disease—or symbolic—preserving spiritual order. A desert tribe that forbids the consumption of carrion might see it as an offense to the gods of drought, while a polar society that reveres blubber might treat its waste as sacred oil for lamps of remembrance. These distinctions make worlds feel lived-in because they link metabolism with morality.

As you trace these flows—energy rising from sun to leaf, waste returning from ash to soil—you begin to see the planet itself as a living organism. Cities become organs that metabolize trade; roads are arteries; ports are lungs inhaling and exhaling goods. Disease, hunger, and innovation are simply symptoms of imbalance. A writer who understands ecology understands inevitability: when a resource dwindles, desperation breeds invention or war. When abundance overflows, decadence follows.

Consider the drama contained in a single crop. If your world's staple grain depends on a narrow climatic window, a shift in temperature could reshape everything from calendar to religion. Famine becomes prophecy; adaptation becomes heresy. Or imagine a magical ecosystem in which energy, rather than being free, must be "harvested" from luminous stones that fade with use. The scarcity of those stones dictates the scale of cities, the range of armies, the arrogance of empires. Economics and ecology are the same word in different languages.

Population and power must always bow to the limits of energy. If a world has little sunlight or magic, its cities will cluster around geothermal vents, luminous fungi, or imported fuel. Armies will shrink, not because of politics, but because there simply isn't enough caloric throughput to feed a million soldiers. This realism grounds grandeur. When readers understand why your empire stops expanding—not because of sentiment, but because of entropy—they feel that the world has laws as strong as its emotions.

But ecology is not just constraint—it is opportunity. A world's energy system defines its aesthetics. A culture sustained by algae farms glowing under dim suns will build with translucence, their architecture mimicking the veins of leaves. A people who rely on wind-harvested spores will weave sails into every aspect of life, from clothing to religion. Even the taste of a world—its spice, its rot, its sweetness—emerges from its food chain. Energy leaves fingerprints on everything.

To make ecology vivid, treat it not as background but as drama. Every hunt, every meal, every harvest is a negotiation with the invisible architecture of survival. Who eats whom is the oldest conflict in existence. When you make that visible—when a character understands that their victory costs another species its niche—you give your world moral depth. The forest stops being pretty; it becomes an argument about balance.

In the end, all stories of civilization are stories of appetite. The rise and fall of kingdoms follow the same curve as predator and prey: expansion, overshoot, collapse, renewal. By giving your world a coherent trophic architecture—an economy of energy that feels inevitable—you grant it life. The reader senses that beneath the dialogue and the politics, something larger hums: the planet's hunger, steady and eternal. And when that hunger speaks—through famine, through fertility, through the slow composting of empires—the world itself becomes a character, ancient and alive.

4.2 Domestication & Agriculture

Civilization began the moment someone realized that a seed dropped near a hearth could sprout on its own. Domestication is the quiet hinge on which all of history turns. It is not merely the taming of animals or the cultivation of crops, but the transformation of human identity itself—from wanderers shaped by landscape to shapers of it. To design a believable world, you must understand not only what a society eats, but *how* it produces its sustenance, and what hidden contracts bind it to the creatures and plants it depends on. Every field, every granary, every orchard is a moral and technological statement—a declaration of how a people negotiates survival.

Each world, whether realistic or fantastic, evolves a distinct suite of domesticates—beasts of burden, fiber producers, food sources, and spiritual companions. Their existence defines everything from architecture to gendered labor. Consider how a single animal reshapes a city: horses demand stables and wide streets, elephants require monumental arches, pack goats necessitate terraces and narrow lanes. The animal's body becomes the blueprint for infrastructure. A people who rely on giant lizards for traction will build ramps instead of stairs; a culture that harnesses flying beasts must master tether systems and vertical docking towers.

Fiber animals and fuel crops also anchor social hierarchies. The herders who raise silk-producing insects become secret keepers of luxury, while those who cultivate oil seeds wield the power of light itself. When clothing, fuel, and transport depend on specific species, entire guilds rise around their control. These domesticates are not just economic resources—they are cultural icons. Festivals honor their births, taboos guard their slaughter, and metaphors built from their traits infiltrate language. In a pastoral world, to insult someone's herd animal might be as grave as blasphemy.

Agriculture rewires the human relationship with time. Foragers live by season; farmers live by cycle. The soil becomes calendar and scripture. In your world, determine how people manage that risk. Terraces built into hillsides show the triumph of patience over gravity, each stone placed by generations to stop erosion and trap rain. Intercropping—planting complementary species together—reveals an understanding of mutualism, where beans fix nitrogen for grains, or magical root plants purify toxic soil. These techniques are not simply "primitive science" but acts of ecological philosophy: cooperation over domination.

Communal granaries are another quiet revolution. They represent trust—the decision to store surplus for future mouths rather than immediate consumption. Once granaries appear, politics follows. Who owns the stored grain? Who distributes it in lean years? Suddenly, food becomes law. Famine ceases to be a natural event and becomes a political scandal. The control of stored calories gives rise to hierarchies of power, bureaucracy, and corruption. Every temple vault or city hall in your world probably traces its ancestry back to a granary.

Seed guilds, those guardians of fertility, are your world's earliest monopolies. They determine what grows, where, and for whom. A culture that treats seeds as sacred inheritance may prohibit export under penalty of death; another that patents or magically binds its seeds may enslave entire regions through dependence. When you write these details, you are not writing agriculture— you are writing geopolitics in its oldest form. Control the seed, and you control destiny.

Cuisine is the sensory language through which these systems express themselves. The combination of ingredients, methods of preservation, and rituals of consumption all encode history. In a humid world, spice becomes necessity—cinnamon and pepper masking the quick decay of meat. In cold regions, fermentation preserves life through winter, transforming not only taste but temperament. The tang of fermented grain or the burn of salted fish becomes a memory shared by every generation, the flavor of continuity.

Food is more than survival; it's diplomacy. Treaties are sealed not only with ink but with feasts. When two cultures sit at a table, what they serve and what they refuse reveal volumes about their worldview. A desert empire that eats only hand-ground flour may see industrial bread as impure; a river kingdom that ferments fish may horrify mountain dwellers with its aroma. Misunderstanding cuisine can ignite war as easily as it forges alliance.

Taboo is the shadow side of cuisine—the border where ecology meets morality. If a society depends on oxen for plowing, eating beef becomes sacrilege. If an animal carries disease, it might be demonized even after the threat passes. Taboos often outlive their practical origins, becoming metaphors for virtue or corruption. In this way, the ecology of food shapes ethics. A culture's moral compass often points toward its stomach.

Agriculture also changes bodies and minds. Settled peoples develop new diseases, new bone structures, and new anxieties. They trade freedom for stability, variety for yield. The monotonous diet of grain eaters leads to deficiency and hierarchy: those with access to meat or exotic spices become visibly healthier, and thus visibly higher in rank. You can trace class through the teeth of your characters. The noble's enamel glows with citrus and wine; the peasant's crumbles under the strain of rough bread.

When you design an agricultural world, avoid imagining perfection. Fields fail. Locusts descend. Floods destroy. Farmers live one bad season away from ruin, and their gods know it. Agricultural rituals arise not from peace but from fear—a plea for balance with the forces that cannot be tamed. Sacrifices at planting time, prayers before harvest, songs to awaken dormant seeds—all of these are technologies of hope.

Domestication, at its deepest level, is mutual enslavement. The animals and plants humans shape also shape them in return. A horse society learns speed and warfare; a rice society learns patience and watercraft; a fungus society learns darkness and decay. When you choose which species your world has domesticated, you are choosing its temperament. Each field, each herd, each hive is a reflection of what your civilization values: endurance, obedience, ferocity, or adaptation. The plow is not just a tool—it's a philosophy carved into soil.

4.3 Pathogens & Medical Ecologies

No world lives without its invisible kingdoms. For every creature that walks, swims, or flies, there are a million unseen organisms riding its breath, clinging to its skin, or blooming inside its gut. Disease is the oldest storyteller, older than myth, older than gods. It has written the fate of dynasties, rewritten maps, and redefined what it means to be human. To craft a world that feels authentic, you must allow it to sicken.

The ecology of disease begins with vectors—the routes by which life devours life. Waterborne illnesses flourish where sanitation falters, turning rivers into serpents of death. Airborne plagues follow trade winds, binding continents in invisible webs of contagion. Vector-borne fevers ride on the wings of insects, changing with climate, breeding in the puddles of empire. Each disease maps the same question in a different language: *How close do we live to one another?*

Urban design itself becomes the immune system of civilization. Sewers, aqueducts, and waste channels are acts of defense as vital as city walls. The richer quarters sit upstream, the poorer downstream—a literal hierarchy of hygiene. In a fantasy world, plumbing might double as magical filtration, powered by purifying sigils; in a sci-fi colony, microbacterial scrubbers could patrol air vents. But every improvement carries moral cost. Who cleans the drains? Who breathes the contaminated dust? Even sanitation has its caste.

The presence of disease shapes taboo. Cultures ravaged by contagion may develop rituals of avoidance: prohibitions against touch, burial practices that isolate the dead, or masks carved with sacred symbols. Over generations, these customs become aesthetic rather than medical, embedded in art and ceremony. A noble might wear perfumed gloves out of fashion, unaware that his ancestors did so to survive. In this way, plague writes culture long after it fades.

Health economies grow wherever fear meets faith. In one world, temples double as hospitals, their priests both healers and record-keepers of mortality. In another, professional guilds of leeches or alchemists guard the secrets of antidotes, selling cures at ruinous prices. A "blood price" might govern the ethics of healing—each life saved must be paid for in coin, memory, or years. Or perhaps a society has discovered vaccination through myth: an ancient ritual of symbolic infection, blending superstition and science. How a world organizes care is how it defines compassion.

The mythologies of disease tell us what a culture dreads most. Some societies see sickness as punishment from gods, others as imbalance, corruption, or even invasion by alien wills. In one region, healers chant to coax spirits out; in another, surgeons carve to release them. The distinction between priest and doctor blurs. When medicine becomes sacred, the boundaries between life and death, purity and pollution, begin to dissolve.

Pandemics expose civilization's architecture of denial. Quarantine islands, though established in reason, turn into theaters of cruelty—where the sick are banished, the healthy pretend virtue, and trade routes adapt around absence. In coastal worlds, such quarantines might become semi-permanent micro-nations, governed by their own laws and black markets. In space-faring settings, entire stations could drift infected, lit by warning beacons, serving as ghostly reminders that progress cannot outfly biology.

At the level of story texture, disease introduces a visceral realism. Use sensory detail: the sour tang of antiseptic herbs, the bitter smoke of burned linens, the rhythm of coughs echoing through closed shutters. Scars and smells become symbols of survival. In some worlds, those who recover bear luminous patterns under their skin—a badge of immunity and stigma alike. In others, survivors gain altered senses or latent powers, blurring the line between cure and mutation.

The interaction between pathogen and population defines the pace of history. When a plague wipes out livestock, famine follows; when it strikes soldiers, wars pause; when it targets children, religions change. Survivors interpret their endurance as chosen destiny, building theologies of immunity. Some even court infection as a rite of passage. In a magical setting, an illness might thin the veil between worlds, creating prophets or monsters. Every contagion leaves behind not just graves but myths.

Disease is also the great equalizer and the great divider. It humbles kings and spares beggars—or the reverse, depending on its vector. In its wake, societies invent both empathy and bureaucracy: registries, healers' licenses, burial quotas. Outbreaks give birth to data, and data gives birth to control. The first census may have been a plague ledger.

To build a convincing medical ecology, imagine the tension between knowledge and fear. Healers experiment on the edge of superstition; rulers weigh quarantine against commerce; commoners whisper that the cure kills faster than the sickness. Each side is right in its own way. Medicine, like magic, carries moral consequence. A panacea that drains the world's energy or consumes rare materials is not salvation but transformation. Every cure alters the balance of life.

In the smallest details—how a city smells after rain, how people greet one another without touching, how healers mark the doors of the afflicted—you can express the totality of a world's philosophy. Health is never just physical. It is spiritual, economic, and political. To understand how a civilization heals is to understand what it believes about suffering itself.

Ultimately, pathogens are storytellers. They reveal the hidden connections between beings, forcing isolationists to confront interdependence and conquerors to face fragility. They remind every creature that survival is borrowed, never owned. When your world acknowledges that truth—when sickness moves through it as inevitably as weather—you achieve a rare authenticity. The world stops being invincible and becomes human, alive, and mortal.

Chapter 5 — Societies as Systems: Values, Status, and Institutions

If geography defines where people live, and ecology defines what keeps them alive, culture defines *why* they believe their lives matter. Every society is an operating system—an invisible set of instructions that tells its citizens how to behave, what to desire, and what to fear. These systems are not invented overnight; they evolve like coral reefs, layer upon layer of inherited choices, accidents, and rituals. To design a living civilization, you must build it from its logic outward: from values to norms, from norms to institutions. The strength of a world lies not in the number of cities or kings you name, but in how deeply its rules feel inevitable.

5.1 Values → Norms → Institutions

Every culture begins with a few sacred ideas—its *core values*. They might not be written down or consciously articulated, but they hum beneath every gesture and law. Purity, honor, ingenuity, obedience, freedom, harmony, survival—choose one, and an entire world unfolds around it. These values shape not only belief systems but architecture, cuisine, and the smallest etiquette of daily life. They dictate how people speak, how they fall in love, how they die. In world-building, they are your civilization's gravity, pulling every action into orbit.

Imagine a society built on *purity*. Cleanliness and sanctity intertwine. Rivers are sacred arteries, bathing becomes ritual, and pollution becomes sin. The upper classes might live on elevated terraces above the "unclean" masses, not just for comfort but to symbolize moral superiority. Laws codify what may or may not be touched, who may marry whom, and how death is handled. A mere accident—spilling wine, touching a corpse, crossing the wrong threshold—could carry social ruin. Art becomes minimalist, architecture symmetrical, and food divided carefully between "pure" and "profane." That same value system, transplanted into another geography or climate, produces a wholly different society, but the logic holds.

Now take *honor* as the core value. The society orbits around reputation and public proof. Every transaction requires witnesses; every insult demands answer. Speech becomes weapon and shield. The duel, the oath, the blood-debt—all evolve as technologies for managing dignity. Bureaucracies adapt to preserve appearances: court scribes record grievances as if they were sacred texts, and verdicts are recited aloud so truth becomes performance. The family name becomes a bank of moral capital, inherited and spent with care. To outsiders, such a society may seem archaic or melodramatic; to insiders, it is simply physics.

If you choose *ingenuity*—the celebration of cleverness and invention—the result is a restless civilization. Laws must constantly adapt to loopholes; education becomes obsession; social mobility is earned through wit. Even crime takes on a moral ambiguity: the trickster is both condemned and admired. Architecture in such cultures tends to evolve organically, improvisationally—streets winding like thought processes, structures built upon older ones without symmetry. Progress is religion, but anxiety is its priest.

Each of these values, once repeated across generations, condenses into *norms*—shared habits that regulate behavior without the need for constant enforcement. Norms are the quiet grammar of culture. You can tell them by what people do automatically: bowing, removing shoes, avoiding certain words, gesturing a blessing before meals. These small reflexes reveal far

more than grand ceremonies, because they are not performed—
they are lived.

For example, if purity is a cultural constant, even architecture
obeys it. There will be thresholds that demand cleansing before
crossing, separate wells for different castes or genders, and
elaborate rites for washing before meals. If honor is central,
you'll find a conversational style built on precision: interruptions
are insults, promises are sacred, gossip is treason. If ingenuity
dominates, the society will reward improvisation even in
manners: informal greetings, flexible dress codes, the acceptance
of eccentricity.

Norms serve as the bridge between inner conviction and external
order. Once codified, they harden into *institutions*—the visible
machinery of culture. Temples, guilds, universities, and courts
are not random inventions but crystallized behaviors. Each one is
a monument to the repetition of a particular value.

A culture that reveres purity might build *ancestor courts*—
tribunals where ancestral spirits are invoked to cleanse disputes
before legal judgment. The process itself is as important as the
verdict: incense, water, recitation, and silence form the
choreography of justice. A society obsessed with honor might
institutionalize *ordeal trials*, where physical endurance or truth
under pain proves innocence better than words. These procedures
are not relics of cruelty but expressions of faith in moral
physics—the belief that the world itself will reveal justice if
pressed hard enough.

Even in a technological or futuristic world, these same dynamics
persist. A culture that worships ingenuity might replace courts
with *innovation guilds*, where disputes are solved through design
contests or algorithmic arbitration. Bureaucracy, in that sense, is
ritual translated into paper. Every charter, license, or seal exists

to reassure citizens that the values they hold dear have tangible guardians.

When writing institutions, think in terms of *procedures and paperwork.* What forms must be filled out to marry, to trade, to die? Who stamps them? What happens when the ink runs out or the clerk falls asleep? Bureaucracy may seem dull, but it is the most revealing expression of culture—it shows how belief survives contact with reality. A world that prizes obedience will drown in forms; one that prizes freedom will drown in appeals.

But no culture is monolithic. The moment you define one value, its shadow appears—the dissenters, heretics, and borderlands where values collide. This friction is the engine of narrative. The frontier between purity and pragmatism, between honor and mercy, between ingenuity and tradition, is where characters come alive. A traveling merchant who crosses from one value system to another experiences not geography but ontology. What was virtue yesterday becomes crime tomorrow.

Regional and class variations magnify this effect. The same value refracts differently through each social stratum. Purity in the palace means ceremonial hygiene and silk robes; purity in the village means avoiding the polluted river downstream. Honor among nobles is fought with duels; among peasants, with reputation at the tavern. Ingenuity in the university inspires patents; in the slum, it invents survival. The principle remains, but expression changes with circumstance.

A believable society contains contradictions that never quite resolve. The priest who preaches purity eats forbidden foods in private. The judge who enforces honor accepts bribes out of "necessity." The inventor who champions innovation secretly fears obsolescence. These tensions are not flaws in world-building—they are proof of realism. Real cultures always compromise between ideal and necessity, between the imagined self and the lived one.

The beauty of constructing societies from values upward is that everything connects. Economy grows from belief: a culture that prizes generosity builds marketplaces full of open bargaining and gifts, while one that prizes secrecy hides trade behind coded gestures. Even warfare reveals ideology. An honor-based army duels its enemies in formation; a pragmatic one uses stealth and sabotage; a purity-driven one fights only under ritual circumstances, perhaps refusing to kill on sacred ground. When values drive action, even battle becomes philosophy.

As you design, remember that no institution stands forever. When values shift, institutions fossilize, resisting change until they either reform or decay. The guild becomes corrupt, the temple becomes museum, the court becomes theater. These transformations reveal history as living geology: layers of belief compacted into marble and parchment. A reader should sense the weight of centuries behind every custom, the ghosts of forgotten ideals embedded in current law.

Ultimately, values are the soul of civilization, and institutions are its body. One cannot survive without the other. Values without structure drift into dream; institutions without values rot into tyranny. The genius of believable world-building lies in maintaining that uneasy balance. A society must seem coherent yet unstable, proud yet uncertain, ancient yet improvising.

When you align these elements—value, norm, institution—you create not just a setting but a worldview. You show readers that people in this world do not act randomly; they act because they believe in something, even when they can no longer explain why. And that is the secret pulse of culture: it endures not through law or fear, but through habit worn into instinct. People don't live in cultures; cultures live in them, shaping their gestures, their speech, their dreams. The writer's task is not to invent these patterns but to excavate them—to reveal, beneath every choice, the silent architecture of belief.

5.2 Status Economies & Class Mechanics

No world functions without hierarchy, whether born of merit, blood, or illusion. Status—earned or inherited—is the soft currency that flows beneath every social transaction. It determines who speaks first, who eats last, who is remembered, and who disappears. Unlike coin or land, status cannot be hoarded indefinitely; it must circulate. It gains meaning only when displayed, deferred, or exchanged. To design a believable culture, you must understand how prestige operates as an economy—one as intricate as trade, yet far more emotional.

Every civilization defines what counts as achievement and what grants esteem. In one, valor in battle is the highest currency, making scars worth more than gold. In another, piety or scholarship determines rank, so the quiet priest or poet holds more sway than the sword-bearing noble. In a mercantile republic, risk itself might become virtue—the willingness to gamble fortune for discovery or expansion. What matters most is consistency: whatever the measure, the entire social order must agree, consciously or not, on what prestige means and how it is earned.

Status can be accumulated in many forms—through feats, favors, lineage, or divine blessing—but its maintenance demands constant expenditure. A hero must display generosity to remain heroic, sponsoring feasts or temples. A wealthy merchant must fund civic works or festivals to keep respectability. Prestige spent wisely reproduces itself; prestige hoarded curdles into envy. The higher one climbs, the more public one's life becomes. To live at the top of a status economy is to exist in perpetual performance.

This transactional quality of esteem manifests in rituals both overt and subtle. Consider how easily social rank is revealed through language. Pronouns, greetings, and address forms act as invisible barometers of hierarchy. In one world, names might only be spoken upward, never downward; in another, titles replace names entirely, creating a society of masks. Tone, posture, and even silence acquire monetary value. A noble's pause carries more weight than a peasant's plea.

Color and material likewise reveal class. The upper echelons of society, even when they disavow luxury, encode privilege into texture. In one culture, certain pigments—crimson from rare minerals, blue from imported shells—may be restricted by law to royal garments. Elsewhere, only priests may wear white, or only widows may display gold. These rules appear decorative but serve a vital purpose: they make hierarchy legible at a glance. In a world where status governs survival, reading such signals becomes instinct. The result is a choreography of glances, bows, and calculated gestures—a daily navigation of social topography.

Even hair, often overlooked, can act as a visual ledger of rank. Length, color, and ornamentation may indicate age, vocation, or spiritual purity. A society might require its scholars to shave half their heads to symbolize humility, or its warriors to braid victories into their locks. In another, only those who have paid off their debts may grow their hair long, creating a living census of servitude. The body itself becomes a document of social position, one constantly revised.

Mobility within such systems—how one moves up or down—is where fiction finds its tension. A world without social movement is static; a world with too much feels weightless. The balance lies in designing believable *channels* of ascent and descent. Some cultures open advancement through service examinations, where literacy or cunning can elevate a commoner. Others rely on patronage, where loyalty to a powerful household offers vicarious prestige. Marriage, too, serves as a marketplace of mobility—alliances brokered as much for reputation as affection.

Frontiers, both physical and ideological, often function as escape valves for those trapped by birth. Colonization, exploration, or military service offers the chance to rewrite identity, though at enormous cost. These edges of society teem with ambition and resentment—the ingredients of revolution. Every civilization needs such margins, because without them the frustrated energy of the underclasses turns inward, eating the core. A believable world will have both the rungs of opportunity and the friction of corruption that keeps most people from climbing.

Credit and leniency form another aspect of status economy. High rank often buys forgiveness, transforming law into theater. The same crime that sends a peasant to the gallows earns a noble a fine or a public apology. This hypocrisy isn't a flaw in world-building—it's the engine of story. When characters learn to navigate, exploit, or subvert these systems, they reveal both personal cunning and the moral architecture of the setting.

Status also interacts with economics in intimate ways. In some cultures, wealth is shameful unless converted into visible virtue—donations, monuments, or marriages. In others, conspicuous consumption itself becomes moral proof: the ability to waste signifies divine favor. You can trace the health of a civilization by how it treats luxury. If the rich retreat into secrecy, corruption festers. If they flaunt excess, decadence blooms. Somewhere between the two lies stability, though always temporary.

The decay of status economies provides some of the richest narrative soil. When the symbols of prestige lose meaning—

when warriors no longer fight, priests no longer believe, or scholars no longer learn—the currency of respect collapses. This creates a vacuum that new values rush to fill. Revolutions often begin not with hunger but with humiliation: when those at the bottom no longer recognize the authority of those above. In this sense, status is as fragile as trust.

Designing a believable class system means writing a world where every character, even the humblest, knows precisely where they stand. Not because someone told them, but because the entire world tells them—through architecture, accent, texture, and gaze. A servant knows their distance from nobility by the length of a dining table, the softness of a carpet, or the right to make eye contact. Every social space, from bathhouse to battlefield, becomes a map of permission. The reader doesn't need exposition; they can *feel* the hierarchy through how people move and speak.

At its heart, a status economy is a drama of recognition. People crave to be seen, to be acknowledged within the moral logic of their society. That craving drives both cruelty and kindness. A soldier risks death for a medal; a courtesan risks disgrace for a compliment; a scholar risks exile for the footnote that bears his name. Status is faith materialized—it requires collective belief to exist. The moment that belief wavers, empires crumble, and new myths rise to replace them.

5.3 Kinship, Household & Demography

If status is the public skeleton of society, kinship is its blood—the private network through which loyalty, obligation, and identity flow. Every civilization, no matter how vast or advanced, rests on its pattern of relatedness. Family defines not just affection but economics, law, and vengeance. It decides who inherits what, who must avenge whom, and who is allowed to love whom. A believable world must treat kinship as a living calculus, one that governs every stage of existence from birth to burial.

Begin with the basic *unit* of belonging. In some worlds, the clan or lineage is the moral universe; in others, the nuclear household or guild replaces it. A *clan-based* society measures worth by ancestry: the deeds of the dead weigh on the living, and genealogies stretch like rivers through centuries. Here, names are heirlooms and marriages are diplomacy. When one person errs, the whole bloodline pays. Vengeance becomes a duty rather than emotion. Justice itself is kinship accounting—blood for blood, dowry for insult, exile for betrayal.

In contrast, a *household-based* system privileges cooperation over ancestry. The "family" may include servants, apprentices, concubines, or even intelligent tools. Loyalty is contractual, not hereditary. Such societies often excel in commerce and adaptation because belonging can be purchased or earned. Yet their bonds are fragile; when fortune fails, love dissolves into litigation. The difference between clan and household is the difference between lineage and ledger, between memory and record.

Property and duty flow along these lines of kinship like water through channels. In patriarchal societies, inheritance concentrates, producing dynastic continuity and gendered exclusion. In matrilineal ones, power hides in domestic spaces—the hearth, the loom, the gossip networks that shape marriages and alliances. In others, kinship might be chosen through ritual adoption or spiritual bond: comrades who share battle scars, initiates who drink from the same sacred cup. These invented kinships are especially fertile ground for storytelling because they blur the boundary between love and obligation.

Rituals of passage mark transitions within this social organism. Birth names, apprenticeship oaths, coming-of-age scars, marriage feasts, and retirement pilgrimages are the checkpoints through which citizens renew their membership in society. Each ceremony grants rights and imposes limits. A child who has not undergone the naming rite may not be mourned if they die. An adult who refuses the initiation cannot inherit land. These rites are emotional as well as bureaucratic; they teach belonging through ordeal.

Some worlds add physical markers to these transitions. Tattoos, scars, or jewelry indicate life stage and status. A society that burns a mark onto the palms of artisans binds identity to craft. Another might weave colored cords into hair to show marital status or fertility. In such cultures, aging becomes visible progress—a biography written on the body. In contrast, cultures that hide or erase these markers often value individual reinvention; anonymity becomes a form of freedom.

Demography—the mathematics of birth, death, and movement— completes the portrait. High fertility and short lifespans produce societies obsessed with inheritance and superstition: every newborn is both hope and gamble. Low fertility, by contrast, yields introspective cultures where continuity is institutional rather than biological—monasteries, academies, archives. Mortality rates shape theology: in a world where disease strikes randomly, gods of fate and luck flourish; in one where longevity is attainable, faith turns inward, worshiping discipline or knowledge.

Migration introduces instability and renewal. When populations move, so do ideas and taboos. Border towns mix dialects, cuisines, and genetic lineages until identity becomes negotiation. Cities become mosaics of kinship systems overlapping awkwardly—patrilineal merchants trading with matrilineal farmers, each interpreting marriage and honor differently. These cultural intersections create both conflict and synthesis, the lifeblood of any believable metropolis.

Housing reveals demography in material form. In high-fertility regions, homes expand horizontally—courtyards filled with generations under one roof. Privacy is rare; conversation is collective. In aging societies, dwellings shrink and specialize, filled with memorials rather than cradles. Migration produces vertical cities—towers layered by origin, each floor speaking a different tongue. Architecture, like kinship, encodes population trends in wood and stone.

The household is also the first school, bank, and clinic. It teaches labor roles, stores wealth, and tends the sick. Within its walls, ideology becomes habit. A child raised in a clan that prizes vengeance learns arithmetic through blood-debt tallies; a child of merchants learns it through ledgers. Thus, demography becomes destiny—not through genes, but through story.

Myth responds to demographic reality. Fertile societies tell tales of abundance and divine generosity; barren ones venerate sacrifice and chosen heirs. A people constantly at war may exalt reincarnation or ancestor worship to justify endless death. In every case, population pressure or decline writes itself into theology. When a civilization begins to fear extinction, its gods become desperate—demanding purity, obedience, or isolation to preserve the few who remain.

The interplay of kinship, ritual, and demography determines the emotional climate of your world. A society where families are vast and obligations many breeds claustrophobia but also security; one where kin ties are weak produces freedom laced with loneliness. Neither is inherently better—they simply produce different kinds of characters and conflicts. The solitary hero belongs to the latter; the tragic heir to the former.

Ultimately, kinship systems are stories told through generations—narratives of who counts as "us." Demography provides the tempo, and households provide the stage. When you weave these together with care, your fictional society gains heartbeat and breath. Readers will not merely see your world; they will *inherit* it, feeling the weight of ancestry and the pull of birthright in every decision your characters make.

Chapter 6 — Language, Writing, and Media Ecologies

Language is not merely a tool for communication; it is a sensory architecture that shapes perception itself. It decides what distinctions are visible, what emotions are thinkable, and what truths can be told without distortion. Every sound a culture learns to produce and every silence it chooses to maintain reveals how its people attend to the world. To build a convincing civilization, one must begin with its music—the cadence of its speech, the rhythm of its pauses, the shape of its breath. Words do not float above reality; they are the weather patterns of thought, shaping everything they pass over.

6.1 Sound & Mouthfeel

The first thing a reader notices about a world is not its geography but its *names*. The mouthfeel of a name—how it moves across the tongue, how it vibrates in the chest—creates an emotional expectation long before meaning arrives. Hard consonants suggest discipline, cliffs, authority; liquid syllables imply rivers, secrecy, and song. The phonetic texture of a language defines its people's temperament in ways that no cultural description can match. To design this texture, you must first understand phonotactics—the internal physics of what sounds can coexist.

A language that avoids clusters of consonants, favoring open syllables like *ka-na-la*, feels flowing and gentle, the language of traders or seafarers whose words must travel the wind. A language dense with stops and fricatives, such as *krth* or *zkt*, feels engineered for command—soldiers barking across walls, administrators sealing orders with precision. Somewhere between the two lies the earthy balance of agrarian speech, built around nasals and vowels that carry easily over fields. The distribution of sound isn't aesthetic alone; it encodes environment. The plains echo differently than the mountains; desert air favors clipped syllables, while humid forests invite breathy vowels.

The physicality of speech—its *mouthfeel*—anchors your world in the body. Harsh languages with back-of-throat consonants may belong to high-altitude peoples accustomed to thin air, while lowland dialects soften words to save breath. Even within one nation, class and context reshape sound. Nobles elongate vowels to signal leisure; laborers truncate them to conserve time. In merchant quarters, intonation bends upward in perpetual bargaining, while in monasteries it flattens into chant. The mouth, in this sense, becomes a social instrument. Each accent is a fingerprint of experience.

From phonetics flow politics. Sound marks belonging. The accent that identifies a border-town trader also brands him as untrustworthy in the capital. Conquerors rename cities not to reorganize maps but to overwrite memory. When one language dominates another, it carries its worldview with it. Words become the spoils of empire. In your world, decide not only *what* is spoken but *who* is permitted to speak it. A conquered people forced to use their oppressor's tongue might still keep sacred phrases untranslatable—a linguistic rebellion that preserves identity.

Politeness systems transform language from tool to weapon. The way one addresses others—through honorifics, evidential markers, or pronouns—reveals the structure of power. In some societies, each sentence must specify how the speaker knows what they claim: "I saw," "I heard," "I infer." In others, hierarchy seeps into grammar itself: there is one verb for commanding a servant, another for addressing a superior, and another for speaking to the dead. These distinctions are not mere quirks; they embody epistemology, determining how people think about knowledge and obligation.

A culture obsessed with deference will fill its language with honorific particles, creating conversations that resemble duels of humility. "Your shadow graces this doorway" might be the everyday equivalent of "hello." In contrast, egalitarian societies may strip language of titles altogether, using blunt address forms that to outsiders sound rude but to insiders signal trust. A shift in pronoun—an unexpected familiarity, a dropped title—can serve as dramatic turning point in a story, a confession disguised as syntax.

Sometimes politeness conceals violence. In bureaucratic states, excessive courtesy can suffocate truth. Officials thank one another endlessly for their "most valued contributions" even as they undermine them. The language becomes a maze where sincerity dies of exhaustion. In oral cultures, politeness might instead rely on narrative indirection: one never refuses outright but tells a proverb about the foolish traveler who carried too much. Refusal hides behind parable. To understand a world's ethics, listen to its evasions.

Loanwords provide the archaeology of contact. Every imported term carries a fossil of encounter—a trace of who met whom, and under what conditions. The word for "sugar" might come from a distant empire's language, hinting at centuries of trade across desert caravans. The word for "weapon" might bear the phonetic scar of conquest. Over time, these borrowed sounds accumulate into a kind of linguistic map: where merchants sailed, where soldiers marched, where exiles found refuge. A reader fluent in these echoes can reconstruct the world's history from the words themselves.

But not all loans are accepted equally. Sometimes, conquered peoples adopt the conqueror's vocabulary but twist its meaning in defiance. A borrowed term for "civilization" might come to mean "corruption." A word for "tax" could evolve into a curse. Inversely, empires absorb the slang of the subjugated without noticing, spreading it through their bureaucracy until rebellion becomes administrative jargon. The trade of words is as political as the trade of gold.

Linguistic borrowing also reveals technology and prestige. In one region, the lexicon of navigation might overflow with foreign names for winds and stars, showing centuries of maritime trade. In another, words for scholarship or magic may derive from a vanished language, suggesting a lost golden age. Even phonetic mismatch tells a story: a word that breaks native sound rules hints at a recent or awkward import. On the page, such inconsistencies can act as subtle clues for the attentive reader.

Consider also how social strata use language differently. The nobility may cling to archaic forms that freeze time—ceremonial verbs no one understands but everyone recites. The poor innovate constantly, coining slang that spreads like wildfire and soon dies. Religious sects invent closed vocabularies to separate the sacred from the profane; merchants blend tongues to negotiate across borders. These linguistic ecosystems coexist like overlapping habitats, feeding and preying upon one another. The capital becomes a rainforest of registers, every market and tavern a new dialect zone.

Sound can even shape architecture and ritual. A city built around echoing canyons will develop oratory traditions designed for reverberation; a desert temple carved from porous rock will breed whispering liturgies. If language is music, then environment is its instrument. The acoustics of a world matter. In stormy regions, short words survive better in conversation than long ones drowned by wind. On open plains, languages stretch vowels to carry further. The climate literally edits speech.

Beyond communication, language defines intimacy. The softening of pronunciation between lovers, the clipped military cadence between comrades, the exaggerated diction of children mimicking adults—all reveal emotional geometry. A single misplaced honorific can end an engagement; a mispronounced vowel can betray an impostor. The drama of speech is universal, and every syllable is character work.

Inventing a language, however partial, should never feel ornamental. It's not about inventing thousands of words but about inventing *attitudes*. A culture's linguistic rhythm is its collective heartbeat. You don't need a full grammar to make readers feel it; you need only to understand how it moves, what it forbids, what it embellishes. A people who live among mountains will likely fill speech with vertical metaphors—"high-hearted," "deep shame," "rising wisdom." Islanders might speak in terms of current and drift: "He washed back to us," "Her temper turned tide." Such metaphors transform the landscape into grammar.

What makes language powerful in fiction is its moral intimacy. When a character switches tongues mid-scene, they shift not only vocabulary but worldview. A spy speaking his mother's language after years of using the enemy's tongue feels the geography of his soul rearranging. Multilingual worlds remind readers that identity is never singular—it's polyphonic.

Above all, remember that language is selective attention made audible. It tells you what a people have chosen to notice. A tongue with fifty verbs for "to see" but none for "to own" carries a philosophy of observation over possession. A language where "we" distinguishes between inclusive and exclusive groups encodes social consciousness at the level of grammar. These decisions are not mechanical—they are metaphysical. Through them, you tell the reader what your civilization values, fears, and overlooks.

When you craft the soundscape of your world—the consonants and vowels, the registers of power and affection—you are not merely inventing speech. You are designing the emotional physics of an entire species. Every utterance becomes a small act of worldview, every accent a history lesson. Readers may forget your maps and dynasties, but they will remember how your world *sounded* when it spoke.

6.2 Scripts, Numeracy & Interfaces

If sound gives a culture its pulse, writing provides its skeleton—the enduring frame through which memory, power, and law acquire permanence. A spoken word dies in air, but a written mark endures across seasons and generations. How a civilization writes determines how it thinks about time and truth. Each script, whether scratched into clay, inked on silk, or knotted into cord, is not simply a medium of information but an ideology in visible form. A script is a worldview laid flat on a surface.

The shape of a writing system governs who can use it. A society that writes with a complex logographic script—a dense forest of symbols requiring years of study—inevitably breeds elites. Priests, scribes, or bureaucrats guard literacy as their monopoly. Knowledge becomes hierarchy. In contrast, an alphabet democratizes language: its few symbols can be learned quickly, making reading a civic act rather than a priestly one. Somewhere between these extremes lie the syllabaries, efficient yet rhythmic, suited to oral traditions. They translate the cadence of song into inscription, bridging music and record.

Each writing system emerges from material necessity. Clay tablets encourage brevity and accountancy; papyrus allows narrative; silk and parchment invite art. On a world where humidity ruins ink, writing may evolve into tactile scripts pressed into metal sheets or grown into living plants whose leaf patterns store phrases. In magical or digital civilizations, words themselves might carry charge—letters glowing faintly as if alive, or rearranging when read aloud. A script is not only a code; it's a physical performance between hand, tool, and medium.

How a world counts is as revealing as how it writes. Numeracy—the ability to quantify, compare, and predict—shapes commerce, astronomy, and even metaphysics. The choice of base system carries cultural symbolism. Base ten suggests a civilization guided by anatomy, fingers as abacus. Base twelve belongs to traders and astronomers, its divisibility prized for measurement and timekeeping. Base sixty, as in ancient Sumer, speaks of cosmic cycles, where minutes and degrees mirror divine harmonies. Even imaginary worlds might choose alien logics: a lunar people may count in phases, a machine race in binary, an oceanic species in tides. The mathematics of a society is the architecture of its cosmos.

Units of measure reveal daily life. A world that measures distance in "days of travel" prioritizes journey over geography. A civilization that weighs goods in "mouths fed" transforms economy into empathy. The more poetic the units, the more human their mathematics. But when units become abstract—bits, lumens, thaumic densities—society drifts from its body. Every shift in measurement is a shift in philosophy. Standardization may unify empires, yet it also erases local knowledge. A conquered region forced to abandon its ancestral calendar or grain measure is not merely adapting—it's being rewritten.

Documents, too, are acts of ritual. The making of a contract or decree is never merely administrative; it's performance. The ink itself becomes symbolic—mixed from rare minerals, blood, or sanctified oils. The color of writing may encode social status: blue for nobility, black for the divine, red for danger or debt. The brushstroke, the seal, the fold of parchment—each gesture transforms words into authority. When a scribe stamps a wax emblem or ties a knot in a cord, they're not only transmitting information but sanctifying it.

Forgery, in this context, is heresy. To fake a document is to counterfeit reality. Thus, many societies surround writing with protective spells or bureaucratic superstitions. Some mark important documents with curses against alteration—tiny lines of text promising madness to those who erase them. Others embed signatures in living materials: a quill feather that changes hue if its ink lies, or paper that decays when exposed to falsehood. These safeguards are less about practicality than about faith in the sacredness of inscription. A believable world understands that paperwork itself can be dramatic.

Think also of where writing happens. In one culture, literacy might flourish only in temples, scrolls wrapped in perfumed cloth and touched by few. In another, graffiti on public walls serves as the voice of the poor, raw and immediate. A society's literacy rate tells you who controls truth. In worlds where literacy is universal, words lose their aura and become currency. In worlds where literacy is rare, each letter glows with sanctity. Both extremes create distinctive aesthetics—either a flood of disposable pamphlets or the reverent silence of illuminated manuscripts.

Even the act of reading can differ. Some societies read aloud, making text communal and oral; others treat reading as private meditation. The difference changes everything about knowledge and secrecy. A book meant to be read aloud uses rhythm and repetition; one meant for solitary eyes relies on introspection and argument. The shift from oral to silent reading, from communal to private cognition, marks one of civilization's deepest revolutions.

In magical or post-technological settings, interfaces extend the logic of scripts. A world might use glowing runes as programming languages for the cosmos, or living documents that respond to touch. Numerical equations could summon energy fields; calligraphy might shape weather. The aesthetic pleasure of such systems lies not in spectacle but in coherence: the sense that writing itself *does* something beyond representation. Every flourish on a page is a command to the universe.

When designing such systems, remember that literacy always produces bureaucracy. Once words can persist beyond memory, someone must store, copy, verify, and interpret them. The script births the clerk, the clerk births the office, and the office births the state. Writing thus becomes the invisible foundation of government. Even rebellion requires its own paperwork— manifestos, decrees, ledgers of injustice. The pen is never innocent; it is architecture in disguise.

A civilization's relationship with numbers and script defines how it perceives both order and chaos. A people obsessed with precision will turn even poetry into geometry. Another that distrusts abstraction may keep arithmetic secret, a priestly art. These attitudes ripple outward into everything—architecture, music, magic. The rhythm of a verse and the grid of a city share the same underlying mathematics. To invent a culture's script is to design its mind.

6.3 Media Ecosystem & Information Flow

If writing is the spine of civilization, information flow is its bloodstream. Every society invents methods for moving knowledge through space and time—its own ecology of media. These systems, from messenger birds to crystal networks, determine how fast a rumor spreads, how long a lie lasts, and how far truth can travel before it changes shape. The speed of communication defines the speed of history.

In worlds before the printing press, news moves at the pace of breath and hoofbeat. Town criers, wandering bards, or merchants serve as mobile media, trading songs and rumors as casually as goods. Information is performative: it arrives with a voice, a gesture, and an agenda. In such settings, memory is the only archive, and every retelling is a reinvention. The spoken word mutates as it spreads, evolving like a living organism. Truth becomes a collective improvisation.

Later come the couriers and relay posts—structured networks where messages leapfrog from rider to rider, torch to torch. Signal towers rise on hilltops, flashing fire by night and mirrors by day. Distance shrinks but remains visible: one can still watch the message cross the landscape, a physical trail of light and endurance. This slowness breeds patience and imagination. People live with the knowledge that news has a lifespan, that every message will arrive late and warped. Delay itself becomes part of culture, a temporal texture lost in instantaneous societies.

In magical or futuristic worlds, communication may accelerate to near-instantaneous speed—telepathic webs, crystal mirrors, scry-nets, data streams. Yet even then, latency remains: misinterpretation, overload, censorship. The faster information moves, the less time people have to test it. Societies of instant connection develop new pathologies—panic, rumor cascades, emotional contagion. Knowledge becomes heat rather than light.

Control of information defines power. A kingdom that monopolizes scribes or owns the signal towers governs reality itself. When news must pass through checkpoints—religious censors, bureaucratic editors, or magical filters—truth fractures into versions. Each region may hear a different history of the same event. The elite curate the archive; the populace trades in gossip. Between the two lies the real world, unstable and alive.

Rumor functions as a parallel media system. It travels through informal networks—taverns, caravans, marketplaces—and obeys different physics than official news. It multiplies in proportion to uncertainty. In societies where censorship is strong, rumor becomes the dominant form of narrative, half truth and half art. People learn to read tone and omission, decoding meaning in what isn't said. Entire professions can arise around this— spymasters, chroniclers, gossip poets—each manipulating the fog of information for survival or control.

Archival culture reveals how civilizations cope with memory. Some store knowledge in monumental libraries—columns of clay tablets, coral carvings, or digital vaults orbiting dead moons. Others embed it in organic media: trees that record history in growth rings, whales that carry ancestral songs, or human oracles trained to remember treaties. Every archive implies a custodian. A monastery that preserves ancient texts wields the same power as a server farm: the ability to choose what endures.

But archives, like empires, decay. Scrolls rot, data corrupts, memories falter. The fragility of storage defines a world's relationship with its past. A culture that constantly loses records becomes obsessed with repetition, embedding history in ritual to compensate. Another that never forgets drowns in nostalgia, unable to imagine new futures. The best fictional societies exist somewhere between—the eternal struggle between remembrance and reinvention.

Information systems also create their own aesthetics. The smell of fresh ink in a scribe's hall, the clatter of printing presses, the shimmer of light on communication crystals—all convey a world's texture of thought. Even the noises of transmission—drums across valleys, bells across rivers—become cultural symbols. To know how a world communicates is to know its music.

Censorship and propaganda, meanwhile, are narrative engines. In every believable society, information is filtered. What's forbidden to say reveals what's sacred. A regime that censors romance fears intimacy; one that censors satire fears laughter. Propaganda fills the gaps with rhythm and color—mottos painted on walls, hymns broadcast at dawn. Truth becomes a choreography of omission, and writers, poets, or hackers become revolutionaries by default.

In some worlds, communication itself may be sacred. Bards could belong to divine orders sworn to accuracy, punished by muteness if they lie. In others, communication might be dangerous—certain names or messages acting as spells that warp reality. A single broadcast could summon storms or madness. Such worlds make the ethics of information literal: knowledge as contagion.

Finally, consider who owns the means of retrieval. In your world, can anyone access the archive, or must they pay tribute to priests or algorithms? Does history belong to the public or the state? A society's freedom can be measured by how easy it is to *remember*. The more restricted the archive, the more powerful those who interpret it. Priests, librarians, and data engineers all play the same ancient role: gatekeepers of continuity.

The movement of information through a world—its delays, distortions, and decay—determines how characters know what they know. It sets the rhythm of plot and the flavor of realism. Messages arriving late create tragedy; messages arriving early create paranoia. Every world, no matter how magical or modern, must have limits on knowledge. Those limits, and the human ingenuity that tries to overcome them, are the heartbeat of civilization itself.

When you build your media ecosystem carefully, you give your world breath. Every rumor, every letter, every echo becomes part of a living network—fragile, noisy, and indispensable. And in that noisy exchange between message and misunderstanding lies the most human thing of all: the desire to be heard, to leave a trace, to outlast the silence.

Chapter 7 — Economy, Logistics, and Infrastructure

Civilization, no matter how spiritual or artistic its ideals, rests on the logistics of movement—of grain, water, metal, and information. Empires rise not from ideals but from infrastructure. A road is worth more than a crown; a well-dug canal outlives the general who ordered it. To design a believable world, you must start by asking not what people believe, but what they can carry, trade, and store. Every economy is a map of constraints—of who has what, who needs what, and how far they must travel to bridge the gap. Scarcity is the mother of story, and logistics is its bloodstream.

7.1 Scarcity Map & Currencies

Every world, from the simplest agrarian valley to the most sprawling interstellar empire, begins with unevenness. Some regions are fat with grain and timber but poor in ore. Others sit atop gold but starve for salt. These imbalances are not accidents—they are narrative engines. Trade exists because geography refuses fairness. The first step to building a functioning economy is drawing a *scarcity map*: not a chart of abundance, but of hunger. Where the soil is too thin, people will invent irrigation or migration. Where forests vanish, carpenters turn to bone, stone, or imported resin. Scarcity shapes innovation more profoundly than luxury ever could.

Each region, no matter how self-sufficient it pretends to be, must have three things it lacks and three things it overproduces. These asymmetries create friction, movement, and interdependence. The mountain realm might hoard silver but depend on lowland grain; the coast might trade fish and salt for inland wool. In a world of magic, the same rule applies: one city controls enchanted glass, another the runestones that power machinery, another the trained minds to operate them. The resulting trade routes—caravans, convoys, airships, or spirit couriers—become arteries of culture and conflict. Where trade flows, so too flow languages, faiths, and spies.

Scarcity determines values, and values crystallize into currency. At its most primal, exchange begins with barter—grain for goats, water for labor—but soon grows abstract. Commodity money, the first evolution of trade, anchors value in the tangible: metal, salt, shells, spices, or even labor tokens. Each carries meaning beyond worth. Gold endures because it gleams like divinity; salt because it preserves life; spices because they compress distance into taste. The chosen medium reveals what a culture finds sacred.

But tangible currencies always face limits. Metal runs short, salt spoils, shells flood the market. When faith in the object weakens, societies invent *coins*—standardized units stamped with authority. The image of the ruler, the sigil of the guild, or the seal of the temple transforms mere metal into promise. Coinage is theology disguised as arithmetic. It works because people agree to believe in it together. The first counterfeit, however, arrives the same day as the first mint. To maintain trust, empires develop hierarchies of verification: moneychangers, assayers, and tax collectors, each feeding on the complexity of exchange.

As economies expand, coin gives way to credit—the promise of future payment guaranteed by reputation. In this realm, trust itself becomes a form of currency. Merchant houses issue letters of credit recognized across borders, allowing wealth to move faster than goods. The age of paper money—or its magical equivalent, perhaps rune-bonds or encoded stones—creates new dangers. Fraud becomes metaphysical: an illusion of wealth conjured by clever accountants or corrupt magi. When too many promises outnumber realities, devaluation begins, and trust collapses like a star gone cold.

In more advanced or arcane worlds, reputation itself becomes the highest tender. Names, deeds, or social capital replace coin. A hero's favor buys more than gold; a scholar's endorsement opens gates that silver cannot. In such systems, gossip becomes treasury, and disgrace is bankruptcy. The collapse of reputation in a society built on trust can cause economic chaos as surely as drought or war. To design such an economy, you must treat rumor and memory as commodities with measurable weight.

Every system of value eventually faces its *failure modes*. Counterfeits, inflation, scarcity shocks, and corruption test the resilience of institutions. A believable world includes not just prosperity but decay—the slow erosion of credibility that leads to crisis. In a desert kingdom, counterfeiting water tokens might spark revolt. In a floating city, falsified levitation charms could crash whole neighborhoods. The fragility of currency is not a flaw of world-building—it's the pulse of it. Readers recognize truth in the instability of systems that mirror their own.

Taxation, meanwhile, is the skeleton that holds a state together. Empires do not thrive on conquest; they thrive on collection. To tax is to measure, to record, to assert that everything—even breath, birth, or death—belongs to the state. The form taxation takes defines the shape of power. In early societies, tithe barns store grain, symbolizing both divine and royal authority. Farmers carry offerings up temple steps, turning labor into ritual submission. Later, excise gates rise along roads, where inspectors weigh carts and stamp tariffs onto parchment. These checkpoints become theaters of tension: places where power wears its most human face—dull, impatient, and bribable.

The tools of taxation reveal a society's technological maturity. A kingdom that taxes by counting livestock depends on shepherds' honesty; one that audits ledgers uses scribal guilds as intermediaries. Magical or futuristic states may use enchanted abacuses or ledger spells—living records that update themselves, humming softly in treasury halls. Yet the more efficient the system, the more total its control. A perfect ledger is indistinguishable from surveillance. Thus, rebellion often begins not with swords but with erased entries, burned archives, or hidden caches of unrecorded wealth.

Currencies and taxes are the twin pillars of civilization, but they are also its most intimate rituals. To pay is to acknowledge hierarchy; to counterfeit is to deny it. Even the poor understand the power of symbols: a copper coin rubbed smooth by a thousand hands is more than metal—it's the ghost of obligation, proof that lives are connected by invisible threads of exchange. This psychological truth underlies every economy, real or fictional. The market is not a mechanism; it's a shared hallucination made solid by repetition.

Trade, in turn, becomes story geography. Merchants are the arteries of narrative, their routes connecting distant cultures and ideologies. Along their paths bloom caravanserais, ports, and border towns where dialects mix and hierarchies blur. Every journey between scarcity and abundance writes its own mythology. The merchant carrying salt through the mountains becomes the ancestor of explorers and smugglers alike. The path of commerce, winding between lack and plenty, is also the path of human imagination.

Currencies are therefore moral instruments as much as practical ones. A religious culture might forbid interest, framing debt as spiritual corruption. Another may treat usury as divine imitation—the act of creating something from nothing. Some worlds might use blood oaths or enchanted sigils instead of coin, ensuring that debt literally binds the body or soul. Such systems allow fascinating narrative consequences: a debtor whose heartbeat accelerates when lying, or whose shadow lengthens until the loan is repaid. The economy becomes mythic without losing its logic.

Finally, think of currency as language. It tells a story about what the society values. Metal coins speak of durability and tangible wealth; paper notes suggest abstraction and trust; digital or magical credits indicate faith in systems unseen. The transition from one to another signals transformation: the move from feudal barter to mercantile capitalism, from mercantile exchange to speculative empire. Each new layer distances the citizen from the object of value, replacing experience with symbol. When your world's economy reaches that stage, it becomes not merely a system of trade but a theology of belief.

Scarcity ensures that no civilization remains still. Every region's lack and surplus propel caravans, treaties, and wars. Every coin minted or tax collected reinforces a fragile illusion of order. What people can move, they can rule—and what they cannot move, they must worship. A road is a prayer to continuity, a mint an altar to faith, and a ledger a mirror reflecting both the glory and the delusion of human control. When you draw your world's scarcity map and imagine the hands that hold its coins, you are not describing commerce—you are describing the heartbeat of civilization itself.

7.2 Networks: Roads, Ports, and Pipes

An economy, no matter how prosperous, is only as strong as its arteries. Roads, ports, and pipes form the nervous system of civilization—the invisible architecture that turns isolated settlements into living networks. Without them, trade collapses, armies starve, and cities rot behind their own walls. Infrastructure is not background; it is destiny in disguise. Every empire that prides itself on law or art owes its existence to the labor of those who paved, dredged, and maintained. To design a convincing world, you must imagine not only how people move, but how movement itself becomes a form of order.

Roads are the first declaration of empire. A royal road is a visible promise of continuity, linking capitals to colonies, shrines to marketplaces, the heart to the limbs. Its paving stones tell a story of power in motion: soldiers marching, tax collectors returning, pilgrims trudging toward redemption. A well-built road is both weapon and scripture, an assertion that land belongs to those who can cross it without fear. In your world, consider the hierarchy of these arteries. There may be grand imperial highways with mile markers carved in marble, seasonal tracks that vanish under monsoon or snow, and secret smuggler routes known only to those who trade in contraband or forbidden texts. Each class of road carries its own mood and mythology.

A royal road might glitter with brass milestones and guarded tollhouses where scribes record every traveler's name. A smuggler's trail, by contrast, may be marked by cairns and coded graffiti, known only to those who can read the pattern of stones. Between them lie the humble farm tracks and caravan paths— veins of local commerce that feed the great arteries. When designing these networks, remember that they are political statements as much as engineering feats. Whoever maintains a road owns the narrative of distance.

Ports, meanwhile, are civilization's lungs. They inhale wealth and exhale ideas. The geometry of a port—its depth, its tide rhythm, its breakwaters—determines the scale of trade and the character of the city that grows around it. A harbor open to the ocean must master the violence of waves with vast sea walls; a river port, sheltered but shallow, must rely on dredgers and pilots who memorize shifting sands. Every port is an argument with nature, and the shape of that argument defines its culture.

Coastal ports built on tidal flats live by the clock: ships can depart only during narrow windows of high water, and entire economies revolve around these temporal gates. River ports, on the other hand, depend on the mood of floods and droughts, forcing merchants to gamble on the weather. In both cases, geometry becomes destiny. A deep bay breeds imperial ambition, capable of harboring fleets; a rocky coastline breeds isolationism, its ships small and nimble. The shoreline is the world's original border, constantly rewritten by wind and current.

Under the surface of this network flow the true lifelines—water and energy. Aqueducts, canals, pipes, and grids form the circulatory system that sustains urban life. An aqueduct spanning miles of desert becomes more than infrastructure; it becomes a monument to faith in human persistence. Entire festivals might commemorate its completion or cleaning. In a steampunk or magical setting, energy grids may replace aqueducts: glowing conduits channeling stored power from geothermal sources or battery monasteries, where monks chant over crystals to maintain voltage. In such worlds, infrastructure becomes civic religion— citizens measure their faith in how brightly their lamps burn or how long their baths stay warm.

Cities express their identity through these systems. A metropolis of canals gleams with mirrored light, every bridge a poem to motion. A desert city might pride itself on the whisper of underground water channels, their secrecy a metaphor for humility. A mountain realm might be defined by its rope bridges and switchbacks, where distance is measured not in miles but in altitude. These details are not decoration; they are the grammar of belonging. Citizens grow to love the hum of their water pumps, the rhythm of the ferry bells, the scent of heated pipes on cold mornings. Infrastructure becomes memory.

The maintenance of these vast systems tells another story—the story of labor, duty, and continuity. A world where aqueducts clean themselves or roads never erode loses texture; maintenance is civilization's most human act. Ancient societies relied on *corvée* labor—mandatory service from citizens or conquered peoples to keep canals clear and roads repaired. Later eras develop guild contracts, specialized groups of engineers, masons, and dredgers whose reputations carry across generations. In magical societies, repair itself may be ritualized: saint days when the populace gathers to scrub fountains or renew protective charms on bridges. Maintenance is a civic liturgy, a moment when the abstract ideal of community becomes tangible through shared sweat.

Infrastructure also shapes social order. Those who control maintenance control continuity. A guild that manages canal dredging can strangle trade by striking; a priesthood that blesses the aqueduct water can withhold purity from rebels. Even the humble tollkeeper becomes a gatekeeper of fate. When writing such worlds, think of infrastructure not as neutral but as contested terrain. The real war for empire is fought not only on battlefields but along roads and pipes—who repairs them, who taxes them, who guards them after dark.

In the end, every civilization must choose between expansion and upkeep. Roads stretch further than empires can patrol, aqueducts age faster than budgets can sustain. The tension between ambition and maintenance defines the arc of history: the golden age when roads gleamed, and the slow decline when weeds cracked the pavement. To design your world's networks is to determine its rhythm of rise and fall, its pulse of prosperity and decay.

7.3 Supply Chains & Bottlenecks

If roads and ports are the body of civilization, supply chains are its metabolism—the dynamic process by which resources are transformed, transported, and consumed. The stability of any realm depends not on its kings or philosophers but on whether bread, timber, and salt can move from source to mouth without interruption. Every caravan, convoy, or warehouse represents an act of faith: that tomorrow the road will still be safe, the pass still open, the merchant still honest. Logistics is the poetry of survival written in ledgers and sweat.

At the heart of every supply system lie chokepoints—those narrow places in geography or bureaucracy where control of flow becomes control of fate. A mountain pass guarded by a fortress, a strait plagued by storms, a bridge taxed by corrupt officials: each one becomes a valve of history. Whoever rents or owns these chokepoints wields disproportionate power. A baron who holds a bridge may earn more from tolls than a duke from fields. In ancient river civilizations, the keeper of locks and sluices often held more leverage than generals. In your world, power will gravitate to those who can interrupt or guarantee motion.

Seasons dictate the tempo of supply. Grain moves after harvest; armies march after thaw; caravans travel before monsoon. The timing of trade defines strategy. A winter siege, often romanticized in legend, is in truth a story of logistics—of dwindling stores, frozen routes, and desperate rationing. To write it well, imagine the fatigue of counting sacks of grain as often as counting spears. The greatest tacticians are not always warriors but quartermasters. Their victories are measured not in blood but in calories.

Weather creates its own calendar of opportunity and peril. Sea lanes open with predictable winds; mountain routes freeze shut for half the year. The anticipation of these windows governs diplomacy and war alike. A kingdom whose harvest coincides with enemy drought gains leverage beyond armies. Even the sky becomes an ally or saboteur. A world feels authentic when its logistics obey natural law—when ships wait for favorable tides, when merchants risk famine by gambling on an early spring.

Risk defines the structure of trade. Caravans merge at dangerous crossings for mutual defense, forming temporary alliances of necessity. Convoys on the sea hire wardens or mercenary captains to repel pirates. Insurance, formal or magical, evolves as civilization's coping mechanism against uncertainty. A merchant might deposit a lock of hair in a temple vault to ensure divine compensation if lost at sea, or invest in "mirror contracts," enchanted documents that shatter when goods are destroyed. The need to hedge risk gives rise to bureaucracy, and bureaucracy gives rise to narrative—the endless correspondence of reassurance, accusation, and debt.

Every link in a supply chain has its rituals. Dockworkers bless the first crate unloaded after storm season. Caravan leaders break bread with rival captains before parting, ensuring grudging cooperation in emergencies. Even bureaucrats participate, stamping manifests with symbols meant to appease whatever gods govern fortune. These habits make commerce feel human; they are the emotional grease in the machinery of trade.

Bottlenecks also appear in less visible places—within institutions and hierarchies. A corrupt clerk who withholds a signature can delay an entire fleet. A priest who refuses to bless grain shipments for theological reasons can starve a province. Bureaucracy, like geography, produces its own mountains and straits. Power accumulates wherever delay is profitable. In your world, a single ledger office could be as strategically important as a fortress wall.

Supply chains fail not only through disaster but through complacency. Roads left unrepaired, warehouses infested, guild rivalries unresolved—all create slow strangulation rather than sudden collapse. Realistic worlds breathe through such fragilities. A flood in one valley becomes a famine two provinces away. A strike among porters ripples into rebellion among soldiers unpaid for months. The flow of goods mirrors the flow of faith: once people stop believing the system will deliver, collapse follows faster than any army could march.

Innovation often begins as an attempt to solve logistical pain. The invention of the stirrup, the compass, the refrigeration spell, or the teleport gate arises not from curiosity but from hunger and delay. Each advance redefines the geography of trade. A teleportation circle might destroy entire port cities by rendering them obsolete; an enchanted cold-storage vault might end the power of salt barons overnight. Progress is not neutral—it redistributes risk, erases old monopolies, and births new ones.

Bottlenecks, however, are eternal. Solve one, and another emerges. Civilization thrives on partial friction; total efficiency kills story. When goods move too easily, meaning drains from motion. Difficulty is the crucible of value. The merchant who crosses deserts, the sailor who braves monsoons, the clerk who keeps accounts through famine—all become heroes of endurance. Logistics, at its core, is human drama disguised as arithmetic.

To build a convincing economy of motion, think of every road, port, and pass as a living organism with its own memory and appetite. Trade routes are stories written in dust and salt; every ledger line is a heartbeat in the long body of civilization. When those arteries clog—through greed, storm, or neglect—the world shudders. And when they run freely again, the air smells of promise. Civilization, after all, is nothing more than a fragile choreography of movement sustained by faith that tomorrow, the caravan will arrive.

Chapter 8 — Law, Power, and Conflict

Every civilization, no matter how noble its ideals or chaotic its politics, eventually faces the same question: who has the right to say "this is justice"? Law is not born from harmony but from conflict—the friction between power and morality, between what is written and what is endured. The existence of law implies the existence of transgression, and in that tension lies the engine of storytelling. For a world to feel alive, its legal systems must not simply exist on paper; they must breathe, contradict, and bleed. They must reveal the space between what a society says it believes and what it actually does.

8.1 Legality vs. Legitimacy

In every functioning world, two kinds of law coexist: the *law that is written* and the *law that is lived.* The first occupies scrolls, codes, and carved edicts—grand declarations of fairness and order. The second lives in whispers, gestures, and backroom deals. The real story always happens in the gap between them. Legality defines the structure of authority, but legitimacy defines its soul. A law may be obeyed out of fear, but only legitimacy makes it feel just. Without that belief, every courthouse becomes a fortress, and every guard a potential rebel.

A believable world understands this divide. In a formal sense, written law claims universality—it aspires to perfection. It declares that theft is theft, murder is murder, regardless of who commits it. But in practice, every society creates exceptions. Nobles receive leniency, priests claim divine immunity, merchants bribe officials, and soldiers commit sanctioned crimes in the name of order. The written law exists to project an illusion of balance, while lived law reveals who actually holds power. To write about law, therefore, is to write about hypocrisy made elegant.

Consider how justice travels through the layers of society. A peasant may appeal to local custom, quoting ancestral norms rather than written codes. A merchant might rely on guild arbitration, trusting peers more than kings. A noble might bypass courts entirely and appeal directly to divine right. Each group inhabits a separate jurisdiction, each convinced its own rules are the real ones. When these worlds intersect—when the guild summons a noble's servant, or a priest defies a royal decree—the clash becomes narrative gold. Every jurisdictional overlap is a fault line waiting to crack.

Jurisdictions, in this sense, are miniature worlds within the larger one. The *temple courts* may operate under divine mandate, judging sin rather than legality. Their trials concern purity and repentance rather than guilt. The *merchant courts* care about contracts and proof of delivery, not morality. For them, a broken promise is worse than a murder, because it threatens trust in trade. Meanwhile, the *crown courts*—secular, slow, and bureaucratic— view both as rivals. Kings fear clerics who claim to speak for heaven, and despise merchants who measure justice in coin. To navigate this labyrinth, clever characters—lawyers, spies, prophets—learn the art of *forum shopping*: seeking whichever court offers the most favorable outcome. A thief might confess before a lenient temple tribunal to avoid the gallows of the crown. A heretic might bribe a merchant judge to classify his rebellion as a contractual dispute rather than blasphemy. Law, at its most intricate, becomes a theater of survival.

The conflict between legality and legitimacy intensifies in times of crisis. When famine strikes or war spreads, the letter of the law collapses beneath necessity. Theft of bread becomes mercy; treason becomes conscience. Rulers respond by rewriting law in their favor, and the people respond by inventing their own codes—black markets, sanctuary zones, vigilante justice. The line between criminal and hero blurs. In such moments, the truest measure of civilization is not whether the law holds, but what rises to replace it when it breaks.

In your world, the mechanisms of proof and punishment give texture to its moral imagination. A society that values reason will favor evidence, witnesses, and measured judgment. One that values faith will favor ordeal—divine tests where guilt or innocence is decided by the gods themselves. Each method reveals a worldview. The scales of justice are never neutral; they tilt toward whatever a society worships.

Proof standards define not just trials but entire genres of story. In a world where written contracts hold sacred power, forgeries and heists become acts of cosmic rebellion. In another where divine revelation decides guilt, heresy becomes both crime and proof. Imagine a courtroom where truth is measured by magic, but magic itself can be corrupted. A defendant might bribe the priest who interprets the gods' vision, or invoke a counter-ritual that clouds divine sight. The trial becomes less about law and more about performance—who can manipulate belief most convincingly.

The evidence culture of a society also dictates its rhythms of corruption. In bureaucratic realms, proof comes in the form of documents—seals, signatures, and records. Those who control paper control reality. The theft or destruction of archives becomes political warfare. In oral societies, memory itself is the courtroom. Elders or bards serve as living repositories of truth, and verdicts depend on their recall. Here, perjury becomes a kind of amnesia: to forget is to sin. Between these extremes lies a hybrid world where truth is both spoken and written, and every contradiction between memory and record breeds intrigue.

When designing your legal systems, imagine the *ordeal technologies* that embody justice. In one culture, the accused may walk across heated stones, their innocence proven if they emerge unburned. In another, a judge might release enchanted insects whose swarm pattern determines guilt. In a mechanized empire, proof might rest on instruments that measure pulse, aura, or tone of voice. Each ordeal system reflects a theology of truth. A society that uses physical pain to test innocence believes that suffering reveals purity; one that relies on machines believes that truth is quantifiable. The tools of justice reveal its metaphysics.

Law is also theater—its rituals, costumes, and architecture signal its authority. The courthouse itself becomes a stage: columns for permanence, high ceilings for awe, uniforms for distance. Even the smallest procedural detail—the bow before a judge, the oath sworn on a relic—reinforces the illusion that law is divine, not human. Yet behind the curtain lies the messy reality of politics and persuasion. Lawyers whisper deals in corridors, clerks accept bribes, guards enforce order with calculated cruelty. The spectacle of justice hides the machinery of coercion.

At its deepest level, the distinction between legality and legitimacy is emotional. Legality is the skeleton of society—rigid, cold, codified. Legitimacy is its flesh—warm, subjective, alive. When the two align, peace flourishes; when they diverge, revolution begins. Every uprising begins with a single shared conviction: *this law no longer deserves obedience.* When that moment arrives, statues fall, oaths dissolve, and the system resets around a new story of justice.

The storyteller's task is to make readers feel that fracture. To show them not only how laws are written but how they are broken, bent, and reinterpreted. The gap between legality and legitimacy is where character arcs bloom: the corrupt official who finds conscience, the outlaw who becomes hero, the zealot who mistakes cruelty for righteousness. Conflict emerges not from good versus evil, but from competing definitions of fairness.

In building a world's legal culture, remember that justice is never an abstraction—it is experienced through the body. Chains, scars, ink, and fear are its vocabulary. The accused kneel, the judge looks down, and the space between them vibrates with centuries of hierarchy. When you show how justice feels—its weight, its taste, its choreography—you transform law from background setting into moral landscape.

Law, after all, is not the opposite of chaos. It is chaos domesticated, caged within sentences and seals, forever threatening to break free. The balance between written code and lived truth defines the soul of a civilization. Every society writes its laws in ink and its exceptions in blood. The wise know that both are necessary—that too much order petrifies, too much lenience unravels. Between them lies the fragile art of governance, where power tells itself a story and calls it justice.

8.2 Coercion Systems

Every government, no matter how noble its constitution or sacred its origin story, eventually depends on organized force. Ideals persuade, but coercion compels. The visible machinery of peace—laws, treaties, markets—rests on the unspoken assumption that somewhere, someone is ready to draw a sword, load a crossbow, or cast a binding spell when persuasion fails. Power may begin with legitimacy, but it survives through logistics: pay, provisions, and fear. To design a credible world, you must imagine how authority is maintained day to day—not just by decree, but by enforcement.

Policing systems, in any age, mirror the anxieties of those who rule. A merchant republic creates watch guilds: men and women paid modestly to patrol streets, keep fires in check, and escort shipments. They operate like craftsmen, wearing the same symbols of trade they protect, yet answer to guildmasters who measure justice in balance sheets. In contrast, a theocracy's peacekeepers—perhaps inquisitors or zealots—see themselves as instruments of divine purity. Their loyalty belongs not to a city but to scripture, and their weapons are ritual as much as steel. A feudal realm might rely on militias, half-trained peasants called to arms when unrest threatens. Their power is local and temporary; they are more a warning to rebels than a defense against them. Each policing model carries its own logic of loyalty and failure.

Oversight—or its absence—determines whether such forces preserve order or become predators. The more distant the rulers, the more autonomous the enforcers. In an empire where roads are long and communication slow, local constables may turn into miniature lords, dispensing rough justice that serves convenience over fairness. In a bureaucratic city-state, accountability might exist through inspection: auditors, secret tribunals, or magical devices that record speech and action. But even perfect surveillance has its price. When everyone is watched, paranoia replaces trust, and compliance replaces faith. A believable world remembers that repression is never free—it must be fed with money, information, and the illusion of righteousness.

Every form of coercion needs infrastructure. Fortifications embody that necessity in stone, wood, and ingenuity. The materials of defense reveal the world's technological horizon. A society rich in labor but poor in metal might build with rammed earth and timber palisades, relying on terrain rather than weapons. Another might master masonry, crafting citadels that double as temples, their stones quarried from mountains and blessed against decay. In magical or advanced settings, fortifications evolve beyond walls: shimmering barriers of force, illusionary decoys, or gravity-warping fields that distort siege engines. Yet every innovation invites its countermeasure. The catapult provokes the bastion; the bastion provokes the cannon; the cannon provokes diplomacy. History in any world is a contest between builders and breakers.

Even the mightiest fortress reveals a psychological truth. Walls exist as much to reassure the defended as to repel the attacker. They project confidence, stability, permanence. When those walls fall, the illusion collapses faster than the masonry. That's why rulers invest not only in defense but in its appearance: polished gates, ornate watchtowers, banners fluttering from ramparts. The theater of strength matters as much as the substance. A fortress that looks impregnable deters more sieges than one that actually is.

Policing and fortification, however, cost more than stone and discipline—they require budgets. Soldiers and guards must be paid, fed, and housed; horses need fodder; weapons need maintenance. A realm that cannot afford its coercive apparatus loses control faster than one that lacks virtue. Thus, the first duty of finance ministers and treasurers is not funding welfare or education, but ensuring that the garrison's wages arrive on time. Late pay breeds mutiny; unpaid soldiers become bandits with better training.

In many societies, rulers outsource coercion through contracts. Mercenary companies, inquisitorial orders, or debt-collecting guilds act as rented fists, saving the state immediate expense but risking long-term autonomy. These private enforcers, loyal to profit rather than polity, eventually grow powerful enough to dictate terms. A city that relies too heavily on hired soldiers will one day serve them. The mercenary captain's seal replaces the crown's insignia, and control dissolves into negotiation. A world feels authentic when repression carries a visible price tag: silver for soldiers, silence for dissent, blood for obedience.

The human cost of coercion is equally critical. To sustain authority through fear corrodes those who wield it. A constable who spends his life interrogating neighbors begins to see every smile as deceit. A guard stationed at a fortress for years without war turns brittle with boredom. Institutions of control breed trauma and superstition; haunted barracks, cursed dungeons, and ancestral ghosts of prisoners become part of the architecture of power. Repression, in fiction as in life, is never sterile—it leaves residue.

Ultimately, coercion is not only about weapons or tactics but about narrative. The legitimacy of enforcement depends on the story society tells itself. Are guards protectors or parasites? Are inquisitors heroes or monsters? Each culture answers differently, and those answers shape identity. Some may ritualize violence as civic virtue, holding parades to honor the watch. Others bury their enforcers in unmarked graves, ashamed of necessary cruelty. The most interesting worlds inhabit that moral ambiguity, where justice and oppression share the same uniform, and where power's endurance depends on convincing people that obedience is safety.

8.3 War, Diplomacy, and Irregulars

If policing preserves order, war remakes it. Conflict is politics made kinetic—the continuation of negotiation by other means. Every world's history, no matter how fantastical, bears the marks of its terrain and its logistics. Geography is the great general that commands all others. The way armies move, the way empires expand, and the way peace is negotiated all depend on the friction of the land.

A flat, wind-swept steppe produces cavalry cultures: nomads whose tactics rely on speed, ambush, and encirclement. Their strength lies in mobility, their weakness in permanence. When such people conquer cities, they struggle to rule them; their freedom erodes under the weight of walls. Mountain nations, by contrast, fight defensively. They turn geography into ally— passes fortified, peaks watched, avalanches weaponized. In jungles and wetlands, attrition replaces heroism. Disease, insects, and hunger kill more soldiers than swords. Here, the concept of victory becomes absurd; survival itself is triumph. Naval powers see the world as geometry—choke points, trade winds, and tides are their battlefield. Their strategy depends less on courage than on mathematics. Each of these landscapes shapes the psychology of its warriors and the philosophy of its wars.

Diplomacy is war by gentler tools. Treaties, emissaries, and oaths are forms of armistice encoded in language. The rituals of negotiation—safe-conduct tokens, gifts, feasts, hostage exchanges—are performances of trust enacted between people who do not trust one another. In many cultures, diplomats are considered sacred, untouchable even in times of hostility. Their immunity is civilization's final thread; to kill an envoy is to kill the possibility of speech itself. Thus, protocols evolve to protect this fragile channel: special cloaks, symbols of truce, passwords whispered to border guards. In a magical setting, this might include sigils guaranteeing safe passage or enchanted contracts that punish betrayal.

Oath enforcement becomes the backbone of peace. In societies where divine powers exist, oaths sworn before gods carry tangible risk—perjury invites plague, madness, or infertility. In secular worlds, the punishment for oath-breaking must be political: reputational collapse, loss of trade, collective embargo. In both cases, enforcement relies on visibility. An oath means nothing if no one knows it was broken. Hence, ceremonies grow elaborate, with witnesses, relics, and inscriptions to bind memory. Diplomacy's power lies not in sincerity but in spectacle.

Every empire must manage not only armies but also those who fight outside the lines—the irregulars. Pirates, rebels, mercenaries, and partisans occupy the gray zone between warfare and crime. Their existence is proof that conflict is economic before it is moral. A pirate may call himself entrepreneur of the seas, taxing the unguarded; a rebel may claim to be the true collector of tithes, redistributing wealth through extortion. In unstable states, these irregulars often act as unofficial agents of policy. When rulers cannot afford war, they fund raiders. When they cannot enforce peace, they hire bandits to terrorize rivals. Violence outsourced becomes deniable, but never invisible.

Irregular warfare thrives on asymmetry. The weaker side substitutes cunning for strength—ambush, sabotage, rumor. Forests, ruins, and sewers become their strongholds. In such wars, time itself becomes weapon. The regular army must win quickly or lose gradually; the irregular only needs to survive. The longer conflict drags on, the more legitimacy shifts toward the insurgent. History repeatedly shows that occupation exhausts the occupier more than the occupied. The same dynamic applies in any world, whether the battlefield is desert or data network.

Economy drives warfare as much as ideology. Armies march on their stomachs, fleets on their timber, mercenaries on their pay. The cost of sustaining conflict determines its length more than strategy does. The most advanced kingdoms collapse not from defeat but from insolvency. Thus, the balance between treasury and campaign becomes the silent calculus behind every battle. A war fought without budget becomes banditry; a peace maintained without funding becomes illusion. This tension between wealth and violence is the heartbeat of history.

Diplomacy, meanwhile, is war's quieter twin. Both rely on logistics, but of emotion rather than supply. Envoys carry not rations but gestures—gifts, metaphors, and calculated humility. A treaty banquet may involve more risk than a skirmish, for words can wound longer than blades. Each culture develops its own code of courtesy. In one, direct speech is seen as virtue; in another, bluntness is barbarism. Misreading etiquette can start wars as easily as espionage.

And then there is the gray world of peacekeeping—the uneasy truce where coercion and diplomacy blur. Victors install governors, train local militias, and rebuild roads under the guise of generosity. Defeated regions simmer under surveillance, their children raised to resent their liberators. Here, war never ends; it only changes uniform. The art of ruling conquered peoples lies not in cruelty but in managing exhaustion—offering just enough comfort to prevent rebellion, just enough injustice to maintain fear.

In every believable world, conflict is cyclical. The same soldiers who once fought as defenders become mercenaries in another land; rebels of yesterday become bureaucrats of tomorrow. Legitimacy migrates, carrying memory with it. Peace, in this view, is simply a pause between reorganizations of violence.

Ultimately, war and diplomacy are two dialects of the same language—coercion translated through culture. Both seek control; both demand narrative. Victories are stories first, facts second. The flags planted on conquered soil, the treaties signed under candlelight—all are performances meant to persuade the living and outwit the dead. What endures is not the battle itself but the myth of who was right to fight. In this way, the law of war becomes indistinguishable from the art of storytelling, each rewriting the world one act of power at a time.

Chapter 9 — Aesthetics, Architecture, and Everyday Life

A world reveals itself not only through its laws and wars, but through the quiet evidence of how its people make, wear, and dwell. Every beam of wood, every stitch of cloth, every wall painted with a mineral pigment tells a story of what the land gives and what the people value. Aesthetic is not luxury—it is resource translated into meaning. Before a civilization can dream, it must build, and every building material whispers the same truth: culture is geology given human intention.

9.1 Material Palette

To design a convincing world, you must first understand its physical vocabulary—the textures, colors, and materials that define its sense of the possible. Aesthetics begins with constraint. The mountains dictate what can be quarried; the forest decides what can be carved; the climate teaches which fibers survive. From these limitations arise the shapes of beauty. The great mistake of world-building is to imagine architecture or art as detached from ecology, as if marble domes and silk robes could bloom anywhere. Style is not chosen—it is inherited from the landscape.

A coastal civilization with little stone but abundant reeds and fishbone will never build like a mountain empire surrounded by granite. Its temples might rise as woven towers of grass and shell, flexing with the wind instead of resisting it. In such a place, strength means suppleness, and the aesthetic of faith becomes fluid: prayers written on driftwood, altars dissolving into the tide. Contrast this with a volcanic realm of basalt and obsidian, where the earth itself seems to hoard heat. There, homes huddle thick and low, their walls absorbing the day's warmth and glowing faintly at dusk. Light becomes scarce and sacred; interiors gleam with mirrored stones or oil-polished floors. A culture built on basalt will prize endurance over grace, weight over ornament.

Every material carries a philosophy. Bamboo bends without breaking, teaching humility and patience; marble endures but fractures under stress, embodying pride and fragility. When you select what a society uses to build, you decide what it worships. The people who work with copper develop a reverence for transformation—it patinates, ages, changes color like skin. Those who work with clay honor impermanence, knowing the same earth that shelters them can be reshaped tomorrow. Even whale bone, that strange composite of strength and sorrow, produces not just tools but ethics: every object made from it is a confession of survival at another creature's expense.

Architecture grows from such moral geology. The shapes that emerge are not arbitrary but responses to material behavior. Stone demands weight-bearing arches; wood invites joinery and rhythm; bone produces curves that mimic the sea. Technology, at its root, is sensitivity to substance. When your world feels tangible under the reader's hand, when its buildings seem inevitable rather than decorative, it gains gravity.

The surface of things—the colors, dyes, and finishes—speaks its own dialect of class and region. Pigments are the veins through which geography enters art. In one valley, red ochre stains everything, from pottery to soldiers' faces, symbolizing vitality drawn from iron-rich soil. In another, the rare blue derived from crushed lapis or a mythical plant becomes the privilege of nobility; garments dyed with it glow faintly under moonlight, a display of wealth visible even in darkness. Each color carries both chemistry and story. Tyrian purple owes its rarity to the suffering of countless shellfish; indigo evokes colonies, trade, and distance. When you show which hues dominate a market or a mural, you are quietly sketching a map of power and exchange.

Dyes also define social boundaries. The poor wear the colors that stain easily or fade quickly; the rich dress in tones that resist the sun and water. An official class system might even legislate these differences, forbidding certain pigments to commoners. Yet, in every society, there are those who subvert the code: smugglers bringing contraband colors, artisans inventing new shades by accident, rebels using forbidden paints as banners of defiance. The visible spectrum becomes a political battleground, a war fought in fabric instead of fire.

The finishes and textures of materials—the gloss of polished horn, the matte of unfired clay, the shimmer of lacquer—communicate worldview more subtly than symbols ever could. A people who prize reflection polish everything to a mirror sheen, turning rooms into metaphors of self-awareness. Another culture might prefer roughness, believing perfection hides arrogance. Even furniture becomes philosophical argument: do you honor smoothness, the erasure of the maker's hand, or celebrate the mark of labor, the grain that resists uniformity?

Repair is the truest measure of civilization's relationship to time. A culture that discards the broken sees beauty as transient and ownership as disposable. One that repairs sees beauty as an evolving conversation between maker and decay. In some worlds, cracks in pottery might be filled with golden resin, the gleam of repair becoming its own ornament. Elsewhere, mended cloth stitched with bright thread transforms utility into quiet rebellion—a refusal to accept loss. Such *repair cultures* encode philosophy in habit: they teach that continuity is not the absence of failure but the art of accommodating it.

In your world, imagine how repair becomes ritual. Craftspeople might hold annual "mending days," where communities gather to restore tools, boats, and garments. Families may inherit not heirlooms but the repairs themselves—layers of restoration passed down like genealogy. Even spells could follow this ethic: incantations that don't erase damage but stabilize it, preserving the memory of imperfection. The resulting objects carry more than function; they carry biography. Each scar tells a story of care.

Decay, too, has its aesthetics. In damp climates, moss and lichen soften stone; in deserts, sand polishes metal to a pale gleam. Some societies wage war against erosion, scrubbing temples daily to preserve their original form. Others welcome weathering, believing that age reveals truth—an ancient statue's worn face seen as proof of its endurance. The decision to fight or embrace entropy defines a culture's temporal imagination. One believes beauty must be defended; the other, that beauty must be allowed to die.

Material scarcity often sparks innovation. A society deprived of traditional resources becomes inventive out of necessity. When wood is rare, builders turn to coral, bone, or even fungus. When stone is scarce, cities rise from packed earth or living roots. These improvisations are not compromises—they're signatures of genius. A floating city built on salt blocks that slowly dissolve, forcing constant rebuilding, might express an entire worldview of impermanence and adaptation. The more specific the material solution, the more distinctive the civilization feels.

Aesthetics always betray infrastructure. The grandeur of a city's public squares depends on its quarries and transport routes; the delicacy of its textiles reveals its irrigation and dye trade. When you describe what people find beautiful, you're revealing what they can afford to waste. Luxury is measured not in gold but in energy spent beyond necessity: carving a column purely for ornament, embroidering a robe no one will see under armor, tinting windows with imported minerals. Beauty, in this sense, is surplus rendered visible.

Yet, beneath every aesthetic lies pragmatism. The ornate balconies of desert towns might seem decorative until one realizes they trap shade and funnel wind. The filigreed ironwork of northern cities doubles as snow filters. Ornament often begins as adaptation and only later becomes symbol. This truth grants realism to your world: no design exists purely for beauty; it endures because it works.

Finally, materials shape the rhythms of daily life. A family living in a reed house wakes to the rustle of walls; one in a stone fortress hears silence. A potter's fingers become polished from years of contact with clay; a metalworker's lungs darken with dust. The sensual intimacy between body and material seeps into language, poetry, even emotion. Love might be described as pliant as wax or as durable as fired brick. Metaphor grows from what the hand knows.

The material palette of a civilization, therefore, is its subconscious autobiography. It records how the world has constrained and inspired its people—their ingenuity, their endurance, their willingness to see beauty in what they have. When you define what your world builds from, what it dyes with, and how it repairs, you are defining its relationship to time, loss, and pride. Every shard of pottery and every stitch of thread becomes testimony. The aesthetic of a world is not an afterthought—it is its heartbeat turned visible, the shadow that supply leaves on the soul.

9.2 Space Syntax & Wayfinding

Every civilization writes itself into space before it writes itself into words. The arrangement of its streets, courtyards, and thresholds is a silent grammar, shaping how its inhabitants move, meet, and think. Architecture does not simply contain life—it choreographs it. A city's design is a social script written in stone and dust, telling citizens when to pause, when to greet, when to keep walking. To understand the aesthetics of a culture, you must first learn to read its syntax of space.

Urban form reveals ideology. A city planned along straight axial roads, each intersection radiating from a central monument, expresses hierarchy and surveillance. Its order implies obedience; its vistas remind every passerby that they are being observed. A more organic city, grown by accident rather than decree, produces intimacy instead—narrow lanes twisting into courtyards, sudden markets appearing where the streets breathe wider. These curving paths conceal as much as they reveal, fostering small solidarities and private economies. In one, authority gazes; in the other, community listens.

Every street plan carries its own tempo. Broad avenues move like symphonies—grand, predictable, ceremonial. Alleyways hum like improvisation, full of interruptions and syncopation. The traveler feels the difference immediately. A straight road demands purpose; a maze invites wandering. In the former, people march to work; in the latter, they drift, negotiate, or gossip. Urban planning thus becomes psychology in three dimensions. The design of circulation—how one space links to another—decides whether a society prizes efficiency, secrecy, or surprise.

The concept of "street grammar" captures this relationship between shape and story. Each element—the boulevard, the cul-de-sac, the bazaar—functions like a verb or adjective within the urban sentence. A boulevard asserts authority; a cul-de-sac suspends time, creating domestic retreat; a bazaar punctuates movement with sensory chaos, acting as both magnet and equalizer. The bazaar in particular embodies democratic disorder. Its scents, noise, and crowding dissolve rank; a noble brushing shoulders with a baker is a political act disguised as shopping. In such spaces, chance encounter becomes cultural policy.

Thresholds—the liminal edges between inside and outside—encode another layer of meaning. They are not merely physical transitions but moral and spiritual ones. Crossing them often requires ritual, a choreography of belonging. In one culture, shoes must be removed before entry, grounding the body in humility. In another, a veil must be lifted or lowered, signaling transformation from public to private self. Bells might hang from doorframes, announcing arrival not to humans but to spirits. Even the simple act of knocking can reveal etiquette: a rhythm for family, another for strangers. These gestures turn architecture into conversation.

In fiction, such threshold rituals control pacing. They allow scenes to breathe between action and intimacy. A protagonist pausing to wash hands before entering a temple is not wasting time but acknowledging the world's moral architecture. To ignore the ritual is to commit transgression. In this way, spatial design becomes an ethical landscape: doorways, bridges, and plazas acquire emotional gravity. A reader may not consciously note that a character removes her sandals before entering a home, but they will feel the weight of respect that gesture implies.

Wayfinding—the art of knowing where one is and where one belongs—extends this syntax into movement. Not every culture navigates by sight. Smells of roasting grain, the texture of cobbles underfoot, or the echo of a fountain at a crossroads can all serve as orientation cues. In some cities, wind chimes mark districts by pitch, their notes rising toward the sacred quarter and falling toward the harbor. Elsewhere, walls change texture: smooth plaster gives way to carved brick as one nears the market. These sensory anchors ensure inclusivity, allowing travelers, children, or those without sight to participate fully in the experience of place.

Soundmarks—acoustic landmarks—can define entire neighborhoods. The morning clang of blacksmiths signals the industrial quarter; the murmur of prayer identifies the clerical district. Over time, these sounds create collective memory. A child who grows up hearing a certain bell will later recognize home by its tone, even after years away. Thus, cities speak not only through sightlines but through resonance. Architecture becomes auditory inheritance.

Texture and scent perform similar work. The tang of tanned leather might cling to the artisans' alley; the sweetness of jasmine to the noble gardens. Even dust carries dialect. Desert cities smell of hot stone and limewash; coastal ones of salt and rot. These sensory details are not decoration—they are mnemonic devices, guiding locals and disorienting outsiders. When you evoke them, you invite readers to inhabit the body of your world.

Wayfinding rituals often intertwine with belief. Pilgrims may navigate not by compass but by relic sequence—visiting shrines in a prescribed order, trusting divine geometry more than maps. In magical or futuristic settings, navigation itself may be semiotic: glowing lines embedded in streets that shift according to need, or songlines sung by guides whose voices unlock routes invisible to others. In all cases, movement through space becomes a form of reading. The traveler deciphers the city as a living text.

Ultimately, spatial syntax determines how people encounter one another and how stories intersect. In a culture of straight roads, characters meet by design; in a labyrinthine one, by accident. The built environment thus becomes narrative infrastructure. When you describe how a city smells, how a door feels under the hand, how the air changes crossing from plaza to alley, you are not merely setting scene—you are writing culture itself, one corner at a time.

9.3 Ritual Time & Domestic Rhythms

If space is the body of civilization, time is its breath. The way a society divides and experiences hours reveals what it worships, what it fears, and how it loves. Rhythm is politics made intimate. A believable world, like a believable person, inhales and exhales through ritual: morning bells, market openings, evening songs, and the flicker of lamps before sleep. These daily cadences turn abstract time into lived texture, anchoring characters and readers alike within the pulse of ordinary life.

Each civilization carves its own calendar out of necessity. Where water is scarce, irrigation schedules dictate hours. Where tides rule trade, moonrise replaces the clock. Even in advanced or enchanted worlds, time is still agricultural at its core—measured by what can be planted, harvested, or stored. The day begins not with sunrise but with the sound of labor: the grind of millstones, the cry of vendors, the first ladle of water drawn from communal wells. Time is born from work.

Daily rhythm reveals hierarchy. The noble's day is marked by leisure and ceremony—meals scheduled around social visibility, not hunger. The peasant's day follows light: dawn toil, midday exhaustion, dusk prayer. In some societies, curfew bells divide safety from danger; in others, night markets bloom precisely when authority sleeps. A city that never darkens cultivates restlessness; one that enforces silence after sunset breeds repression. By describing when streets empty or fill, you reveal the invisible laws that govern them.

Weekly or seasonal cadences create longer arcs of emotion. Markets might convene every seventh day, drawing distant villages into temporary communion. Bathhouses may open only on lunar eves, turning cleanliness into collective celebration. Religious calendars braid with civic ones, producing festivals where faith and economy merge. In these moments, joy becomes organized—sanctioned release that both unites and controls. A ruler who knows when to give his people a holiday prevents revolt as efficiently as any army.

The heartbeat of domestic life—its cooking, cleaning, and intimacy—depends on technology. A world with open hearths smells of smoke and soot; one with ceramic stoves smells of precision and privacy. The introduction of the chimney reshapes architecture, just as plumbing reshapes gender roles. Who fetches water, who tends the fire, who owns light—all determine who holds power inside the home. A single innovation can invert centuries of habit: gaslight allows reading after dark; hot water shortens ritual ablutions; refrigeration dissolves dependence on salt and ice merchants. Technology, in its quiet way, alters morality.

Baths, in particular, reveal philosophy. Communal bathing cultures understand the body as social property, an instrument of fellowship. Private baths express individualism and modesty. In magical settings, bathing might cleanse aura as much as skin, linking hygiene to metaphysics. The temperature of water, the scent of soap, the architecture of privacy—all become moral signals. Through these details, you show not just how people live but how they believe they ought to.

Light, too, governs rhythm. In pre-industrial worlds, the coming of darkness divides existence into two lives: the public, diurnal one of labor, and the nocturnal one of secrets. Candlelight transforms space, collapsing distance, creating intimacy or menace. In advanced or enchanted societies where night is banished, insomnia becomes cultural. Eternal daylight breeds anxiety, erasing the boundary between work and rest. To design a world's lighting is to design its consciousness.

Festivals knit private rhythm into public order. Harvest feasts bind gratitude to survival; solstice fires mark the turning of seasons; celestial alignments invite awe and taxation alike. Rulers understand that spectacle is policy—crowds gathered to celebrate are easier to count, feed, and indoctrinate. Even rebellion often begins at festivals, when anonymity blooms in masks and noise. These events are both liberation and leash, joy that renews loyalty. A calendar without celebration is tyranny; one with too many is decay.

Ritual time extends into architecture. Public squares double as processional routes; temple steps align with sunrise on holy days. Streets widen for parades, then narrow into alleys of daily commerce. Domestic interiors mirror this rhythm in miniature. Courtyards catch morning light for breakfast, shaded verandas welcome evening gossip. Even the design of beds or dining arrangements reveals temporal choreography—where people gather, how long they linger, who eats first, who sleeps last.

The pulse of time also governs emotion. Lovers meet by market bells; arguments erupt when bread is scarce. When you show the timing of events—the precise hour of dusk prayer or the chill before dawn—you bind narrative to the world's heartbeat. The more specific the rhythm, the more believable the setting. Time, after all, is not universal; it is culture made measurable.

In designing these cadences, think of how interruption feels. What happens when the water doesn't flow at its appointed hour, or when the prayer bell falls silent? Routine, once broken, reveals dependence. A society's fragility hides in the gaps between rituals. The blackout, the delayed market, the cancelled festival—each exposes how much order relies on repetition. Readers sense reality not through invention but through predictability, and the sudden absence of it.

Domestic rhythm is the smallest unit of civilization's poetry. It is the creak of floorboards at dawn, the hum of a market at noon, the whisper of cooling stone at dusk. Through these patterns, people understand who they are and when they belong. When a writer captures that cadence—the sequence of gestures that mark a day—the fictional world ceases to be an idea and becomes a place where someone could actually live.

Ritual and rhythm bind time to identity. They turn survival into habit, habit into meaning. In every world that endures, the sacred hides inside the ordinary: the folding of a blanket, the striking of a match, the smell of bread at twilight. Civilization does not exist in monuments or laws alone, but in the unremarkable grace of repetition—the quiet choreography that makes each dawn feel deserved.

Chapter 10 — Narrative Interfaces, Consistency Ops, and Retcon Policy

World-building, when done well, is not a spectacle—it is an interface. The reader does not step into your imagined civilization all at once, dazzled by encyclopedic detail; they *log in* through emotion, curiosity, and sensory footholds. Every story is a negotiation between disclosure and restraint, between the logic of the world and the rhythm of narrative. The task is not to overwhelm the reader with knowledge but to invite them to participate in the act of discovery. To build a living world is to design how it *feels* to enter it, how it reveals itself, and what it withholds. The machinery of lore must exist, but it must hum behind the walls—audible, not visible.

10.1 Story API: How Readers Access the World

A story, like a city, must have its gates. The *Story API*—your method of access—determines which gates are open, which are guarded, and which are glimpsed only from afar. Readers do not demand omniscience; they crave coherence. They want to sense that, behind the scenes, the world is consistent enough to outlive the plot, but mysterious enough to feel infinite. The balance between immersion and intrigue depends entirely on how information flows. The writer becomes both architect and systems engineer, managing exposition like voltage—too weak and the world flickers; too strong and the circuit burns.

One of the most elegant ways to feed readers context is through *artifact narration*—the use of in-world objects, inscriptions, or fragments of history embedded in the story's surface. A letter, a mural, a travel brochure, a spell manual, a courtroom transcript: these things perform double duty, advancing plot while hinting at infrastructure. They let the world speak for itself without the author stepping in to lecture. A single piece of graffiti can reveal class tension; a weathered decree on a wall can hint at a long-forgotten war. The trick lies in treating these artifacts not as background decoration but as living interfaces—evidence of the system your characters inhabit.

In some cases, the artifact becomes unreliable or incomplete, allowing readers to act as archaeologists. They assemble truth from fragments, feeling rewarded for connecting what's left unsaid. This mirrors the way humans experience real history: partially, emotionally, through what time spares. When the reader encounters a relic or document that isn't immediately explained, they subconsciously accept that the world existed before the story began. The fragment is more powerful than the manual because it acknowledges loss.

Another form of access is *embedded pedagogy*—learning through the novice's eyes. The apprentice, initiate, or newcomer allows exposition to flow naturally without sounding like explanation. They ask the questions the reader would ask but with stakes attached to the answer. Yet this device must be handled with care. The apprentice's ignorance must feel earned; their questions should arise from necessity, not convenience. The reader senses when curiosity becomes contrivance. Let them watch understanding dawn slowly, unevenly, like light creeping into a closed room.

While exposition gives structure, the *negative space* of the world provides resonance. What is *not* explained defines the boundary of myth. When you show a ritual without clarifying its doctrine— when you let the protagonist kneel, whisper, and rise, and then move on—you invite the reader to fill the silence. They do not need to know what god receives the prayer, only that the gesture matters. Mystery is not vagueness; it is precision withheld. Every world must leave dark corners where imagination breathes.

The best negative space feels purposeful, not evasive. It teases connection rather than abandoning it. For instance, a feast might end with everyone turning their cups upside down for a moment of silence. You never explain why, but later, when a character refuses the gesture, the reader realizes its significance through rupture. Meaning emerges not through exposition but through contrast. The act of omission becomes a narrative engine.

Writers often fear under-explaining, but readers are wired to infer patterns. As long as the emotional stakes are clear, the mind will fill gaps automatically. The secret is to imply systems through consequence. If a society forbids travel after sunset, show what happens to those who defy it; don't lecture about the rule's origin. The reaction reveals the structure better than the decree. Let behavior replace explanation, ritual replace taxonomy.

The question of *jargon surface area*—how many unfamiliar terms a reader must learn to stay afloat—is the invisible engineering challenge of immersion. Each new word functions as a gate: too many too fast, and readers feel locked out; too few, and the world flattens into sameness. The ideal balance is evolutionary. Introduce one or two new terms per scene, each tethered to sensory experience. A "skirlpipe" becomes comprehensible when described as shrieking under a musician's calloused hands. The reader doesn't need a glossary if they can feel what a word means before they know it.

Language is an emotional technology. A term that appears mysterious at first should eventually feel natural, not because it has been explained, but because it has been lived. Think of how a traveler absorbs local idiom—meaning inferred from context, not instruction. Over time, words like "tithepost" or "windwall" should cease to feel foreign, signaling that the reader has become a temporary citizen of your world. Each new piece of terminology must justify its existence by enriching texture rather than inflating jargon for its own sake.

Sensory grounding protects the reader from linguistic vertigo. Anchor every unfamiliar concept in the physical: the smell of ink from the decree, the ache of lifting a ceremonial weapon, the hiss of a forbidden machine. The body becomes translation device. When the senses lead, understanding follows. Even the most abstract magic or alien technology gains credibility when paired with tangible reaction—a bruise, a spark, a chill. A well-grounded world explains itself through the skin.

Exposition should also breathe with rhythm. Information delivered in bursts must be balanced by quiet scenes of absorption, moments where the reader catches up emotionally before another layer unfolds. A story that lectures exhausts; one that whispers invites pursuit. The art lies in distributing density. Consider exposition as a seasoning rather than a sauce—it enhances, never smothers. When you reach for a moment of revelation, make sure it coincides with emotional turning points. Readers remember knowledge when it changes the fate of someone they care about.

In complex worlds, information can be layered like sediment. Surface facts—currency names, rank titles—float first, carried by dialogue and texture. Deeper layers—cosmology, philosophy, metaphysics—settle slowly through implication. The reader digs naturally as curiosity deepens. This stratified approach mirrors the real way humans encounter culture: first through gesture, then habit, then ideology. Resist the urge to hand over the entire geological map; let them excavate with pleasure.

Equally important is the tone of authority. The world must sound certain even when mysterious. When a character refers to an unfamiliar custom as if it's obvious, readers accept it. When the author apologizes for the oddity, trust collapses. Confidence, not clarity, sells authenticity. Present your world as though it existed long before the reader arrived and will continue after they leave. That sense of endurance—the illusion of an independent system—transforms exposition into immersion.

The *interface* between reader and world is also a matter of ethics. How much do you demand they adapt, and how much do you accommodate? Worlds that welcome outsiders often lose their internal strangeness; worlds that refuse to translate risk alienation. The balance depends on theme. A story about assimilation should challenge comprehension; a story about belonging should reward it. The key is consistency: once the reader learns the rhythm of your world's difficulty, keep it steady. They can climb any wall, as long as the bricks stay the same size.

Finally, remember that access itself can be narrative. The reader's gradual literacy in the world mirrors the protagonist's evolution. Confusion at the start can transform into fluency by the end, giving the story a structural arc of comprehension. This creates a subtle emotional satisfaction—the joy of mastery. When readers realize they now understand terms and customs that once bewildered them, they feel not taught but initiated. That sensation—of crossing from outsider to insider—is one of the purest forms of immersion fiction can offer.

The craft of exposition, then, is the craft of hospitality. You invite strangers into a house full of unfamiliar objects and expect them to feel at home without rearranging the furniture. To achieve this, you must design doorways of curiosity, hallways of implication, and rooms of reward. Hide the scaffolding—the effort, the rules, the glossaries—but never hide the structure. Let readers feel the weight of architecture beneath the prose, even if they never see the blueprint. The true mark of mastery is when your world feels vast enough to explore, yet intimate enough to trust.

10.2 Consistency Operations

No matter how beautiful or intricate a world may be, it can collapse under the smallest fracture of logic. Consistency is the architecture beneath illusion—the invisible math that keeps faith between the writer and the reader. A single miscounted day in a voyage, a character using a tool before it was invented, a spell that works one way in chapter three and another in chapter nine—these fissures break immersion faster than weak prose. Continuity is not glamour, yet it is the spine of credibility. A reader forgives eccentricity, even implausibility, but never contradiction.

Maintaining consistency across a large or evolving fictional universe is not a creative constraint but a form of discipline, a craft of memory. The more vast your setting, the more necessary it becomes to build what might be called a *Canon Ledger*—a living, breathing archive of the world's measurable laws. This ledger is not for show; it is the engineer's blueprint beneath the cathedral of story. It keeps track of the things that seem trivial until they suddenly matter: distances between cities, the number of moons visible from a given hemisphere, the caloric needs of soldiers in winter, the exchange rate between copper and silver. These are the quiet metrics of believability.

When you first create this ledger, it feels mechanical. But as the draft grows, you realize it functions like a nervous system, coordinating tone and scale. If your magic can only raise the dead once per century, that limitation defines not only plot but philosophy. If a river crossing takes three days, that time delay shapes suspense. Fiction becomes physics disguised as narrative. The ledger anchors imagination to cause and effect. Each note entered—each constraint accepted—adds texture rather than removes freedom. A world with edges feels larger than one without.

The ledger must evolve as quickly as the story. After each revision, every factual ripple should be logged: an updated travel route, a new measurement for a fortress wall, a revised lifespan of dragons. This seems tedious, but it's far easier to repair an inconsistency in notes than in printed text. The act of documentation forces attention, revealing patterns before they betray you. Many writers discover that their best ideas arise not from invention but from noticing the harmonies already encoded in their own notes.

Once the world's laws are recorded, they must be *tested.* Continuity is not static; it is stress-tested by story structure. Each act of a narrative presents different kinds of strain. A heist compresses time and geography; a siege stretches logistics and morale; a legal conflict tests precedent and ideology. Before polishing prose or deepening character arcs, the world itself must pass these simulations. Could the caravan actually reach the city in time? Would a jury system of that culture accept divine testimony? Could an army of that size sustain itself on the available grain stores? These are not distractions from art—they are the mechanics of immersion.

A writer who subjects their world to stress tests learns humility and power at once. You discover how easily grandeur breaks under arithmetic. A journey that should take six months cannot be accomplished overnight without consequence; a population of ten thousand cannot support twenty thousand horses. Yet these realizations strengthen narrative rather than weaken it. When you obey the gravity of your own creation, tension feels earned, victory feels miraculous. The reader no longer senses authorial manipulation, only fate within design.

Consistency operations also require human oversight. No one, not even the most meticulous creator, can maintain full awareness of every thread across drafts. Establish a continuity role—whether in yourself, a trusted reader, or a collaborator. Their responsibility is not to critique prose but to catch reality leaks: the wrong season, the reversed surname, the contradictory political alliance. They serve as your in-world accountant, balancing the ledger of truth. When done well, this role becomes an act of love: a defense of coherence against the entropy of inspiration.

To support this process, keep *diff logs*—records of what changes and why. Each alteration, however small, should carry a rationale. If you move a battle from spring to autumn, note its new agricultural implications. If you shorten the reign of a king, adjust the generation gap between descendants. The goal is not perfection but accountability. Fictional history, like real history, depends on traceability. Readers sense when the writer has thought beyond the sentence, when every adjustment has consequences cascading through time.

At its highest level, consistency management becomes almost liturgical. Each detail must harmonize with the whole. The shape of a window echoes the cosmology of the religion that built it; the form of a coin mirrors the philosophy of the ruler who minted it. To maintain such harmony, one must cultivate a certain reverence. Continuity is a promise: that the world will behave according to its own laws, not bend to convenience. The reader, consciously or not, tests this promise with every page. A single betrayal—a door that opens when it should be locked—shatters it.

World-building without consistency is a labyrinth without walls. But a well-kept canon ledger transforms chaos into coherence. It allows the writer to dream freely within boundaries, to improvise without fear of collapse. Consistency operations are not bureaucracy; they are faith made procedural—the belief that imagination deserves architecture strong enough to bear its weight.

10.3 Retcon Ethics & Version Control

Even the most careful worlds evolve. A story expands, a series matures, and what once seemed absolute begins to wobble under the pressure of new meaning. This is where the delicate art of retcon—retroactive continuity—enters. To retcon is to rewrite reality without breaking trust. It is narrative surgery performed while the patient is awake. The writer must adjust history without invalidating emotion, revise events without erasing consequence. Every retcon, no matter how small, carries moral weight.

A healthy world-building practice begins with a *retcon policy*— an internal charter defining what can change, what cannot, and what must be confessed. Not every error deserves repair; not every contradiction requires correction. Some mistakes grow into myth. Readers are far more forgiving of complexity than they are of erasure. The rule is simple: you may reframe, but not revoke. Rename a town if it clarifies geography; realign a timeline if it restores plausibility—but do not undo death, cancel trauma, or invalidate revelation unless the story itself is about memory's deception.

Each alteration incurs a cost, whether diegetic or emotional. A small correction can pass silently, but major revisions demand transparency. In published works, this might take the form of an author's note acknowledging evolution; in serial narratives, it might become part of the lore itself—a historical discrepancy debated by scholars within the world. The moment the writer treats correction as narrative rather than apology, the retcon becomes art instead of error.

Preservation is the second pillar of ethical revision. Never overwrite a decision without preserving its prior version. Keep branching files labeled by arc or date, ensuring that each fork of the world remains accessible. This not only protects continuity but allows creative archaeology. Sometimes the discarded draft contains seeds of future brilliance—a character motive or cultural detail forgotten in the rush to consistency. The past, even fictional, must be archived rather than erased. Deletion is amnesia; preservation is evolution.

Contradictions are inevitable, especially across long series or shared universes. The challenge lies in how you explain them. The clumsiest solution is authorial fiat—declaring, outside the narrative, that an event "didn't happen" or "was corrected." Such gestures feel like broken immersion, a hand reaching through the illusion to rearrange the stage. A more elegant solution is *diegetic patching*: let the contradiction exist within the world, reinterpreted by its inhabitants. One chronicler calls the battle victory, another names it massacre; one religion canonizes a saint, another calls her a fraud. Truth becomes plural, not flawed.

This method mirrors reality's own imperfections. History in the real world is a mosaic of biases, accidents, and competing narratives. By embracing this multiplicity, fiction gains depth. Readers are not alienated by inconsistency if they can see its human or political cause. A conflicting account becomes evidence of life, not laziness. The retcon, reframed as myth-making, enriches rather than retracts.

The danger of unchecked retconning lies in entropy. Every revision ripples backward, altering cause and effect, diluting stakes. If magic rules change every book, or if mortality reverses at whim, the world becomes frictionless, meaningless. The reader loses faith in consequence. To prevent this decay, treat continuity as gravity—bending is allowed, but breaking collapses orbit. Revision must feel like discovery, not contradiction. When done skillfully, it gives the illusion that the truth was there all along, merely obscured until the right perspective revealed it.

Retcon ethics also touch the writer's relationship to their earlier self. The temptation to rewrite out of embarrassment—to erase outdated ideas, naive politics, or imperfect craft—is strong. Yet integrity demands acknowledgment of growth, not disavowal. Your old drafts are fossils of thought. They remind both you and your readers that worlds, like creators, evolve. When you revise, do so with respect for the mind that built the foundation you now improve. Humility is the hidden virtue of consistency.

In collaborative worlds—shared franchises, game universes, serialized media—version control becomes not only ethical but logistical. Each contributor must know which continuity strand they inhabit, which facts are canonical and which experimental. The use of tags, changelogs, and explicit version numbers transforms chaos into conversation. The document becomes a living organism, its lineage traceable. When readers later encounter discrepancies, they can trace the genealogy of ideas rather than blame carelessness.

Retconning, at its best, becomes a philosophy of adaptation. It acknowledges that no world remains static, that perfection is less believable than persistence. Every living story accumulates sediment—revisions, contradictions, reinterpretations—like geological layers. The writer's task is not to erase erosion but to shape it into landscape. Readers do not need immaculate continuity; they need emotional truth that survives evolution.

When handled with grace, retcon becomes indistinguishable from revelation. The writer appears not to revise but to uncover—peeling back a misunderstanding, revealing a hidden thread that was there all along. The illusion is total: history feels self-healing. But this illusion depends on restraint. The more visibly you tinker, the weaker the magic. Revision should feel like archaeology, not surgery.

Ultimately, continuity is a covenant between creator and audience: I will change, but I will remember. The canon ledger preserves the facts; the retcon policy preserves the faith. Together they ensure that the reader's trust endures through every update, edition, and translation. Fiction is not fragile because it changes—it is fragile because it forgets why it changed. The ethics of retcon remind us that a world, once shared, belongs not only to its author but to every mind that believed in it. Revision is not betrayal when it deepens belief. The true art lies in making every correction feel like destiny—inevitable, invisible, and true.

Printed by Libri Plureos GmbH in Hamburg, Germany